TEACHER'S GUIDE

Everybody's Somebody's Lunch

THE ROLES OF
PREDATOR & PREY
in Nature

Cherie Mason

Judy Kellogg Markowsky

Illustrations by Rosemary Giebfried

TILBURY HOUSE, PUBLISHERS
Gardiner, Maine

TILBURY HOUSE, PUBLISHERS

132 Water Street
Gardiner, Maine 04345

Design & Layout	Rosemary Giebfried, Bangor, ME
Illustration	Rosemary Giebfried, Bangor, ME
Editorial & Production	Jennifer Elliott
	Barbara Diamond
	Mackenzie Dawson
Printing & Binding	InterCity Press, Rockland, MA

□

□

Table of Contents

Chapter Activities

Here is a list of informative and educational activities that correspond with each chapter:

Acknowledgements

When the idea for a children's book on the unlikely subject of animal-eating predators was mentioned to Jennifer Elliott of Tilbury House, Publishers, she didn't hesitate for a moment in giving her support. In fact, it was agreed from the start that *Everybody's Somebody's Lunch* must have an accompanying Teacher's Guide to expand on the subject of predators and their prey to let students know that predators aren't just wolves, they are songbirds, too. So we thank Jennifer for her initial encouragement as well as Barbara Diamond, Jolene Collins, Diane Vinal, and Will Hoch at Tilbury House for bringing both books to life.

In gathering from the immense store of information on predators, we spoke with so many groups and organizations devoted to predator advocacy that our spirits were lifted. We have listed the ones we know about in the Resources sections at the end of this book. There are many more at the grassroots level that are easy to locate by contacting local environmental organizations.

We particularly want to thank everybody at the Predator Project in Montana for invaluable information on forest carnivores.

Since coyotes are a species greatly misunderstood, we are grateful for permission to borrow from the new "Coyote Kit" prepared by the Society for the Prevention of Cruelty to Animals of British Columbia. Also, we are indebted to the publishers of *KIND News*, the National Association for Humane and Environmental Education, who have generously allowed us to include several of their excellent activities on snakes, spiders, and other predators.

Mark A. McCollough, Director of the Endangered Species program in the Maine Department of Inland Fisheries and Wildlife, gave us the address for an international organization devoted to protecting amphibians (the address is in the Teaching Resources section at the end of this book). We also learned from him that there probably is no national advocacy group for individuals concerned with the welfare of reptiles and amphibians. That is a real pity.

Daniel T. Jennings, Ph.D., Principal Research Entomologist, USDA, Forest Service (Ret.), and Cynthia A. Jennings, Librarian, Orono Public Library, Orono, Maine, graciously provided the extensive list of books about spiders that you will find in the More Books About Predators and Prey section at the end of this book.

We deeply appreciate the many helpful suggestions from John W. Grandy, Ph.D., Senior Vice President for Wildlife and Habitat Protection at the Humane Society of the United States, and for his choosing to have both of our books included in their catalog.

Special thanks to our illustrator, Rosemary Giebfried, not only for her extraordinary artistic talent but also for her virtuosity on the computer. She has taught us so much.

Our thanks, too, to the National Wildlife Federation for permission to borrow from "When Carnivores Clash," written by Gary Turbak for the June/July 1998 issue of *National Wildlife Magazine*; and to Gordon L. Kirkland, Jr., Ph.D., Shippensburg University, Shippensburg, Pennsylvania, who gave us invaluable information on shrews.

Finally, we would not be in print without the accuracy approvals of Malcolm L. Hunter, Ph.D., Professor of Wildlife Resources and Libra Professor of Conservation and Biology, University of Maine at Orono; and Kenneth L. Crowell, Ph.D., Professor Emeritus of Biology, St. Lawrence University, Canton, New York.

Thank you all.

Introduction

If our best hopes are realized, *Everybody's Somebody's Lunch* and this Teacher's Guide will take the teacher, the parent, and children into a new century of relating to wildlife. Left behind will be the old idea of "good" and "bad" animals.

Fortunately, we are moving toward a new and broader view of nature where humans are seen as part of an immense working ecosystem where we are deeply interconnected with all life on earth. We are beginning to understand that if the whole of nature is good, no single part can be bad.

Predators, in particular, are overdue for some good press. They have evoked some of our most powerful emotions, from contempt and loathing to outright terror. Consequently, predators, including birds of prey, have been shot, poisoned, and trapped, some out of existence.

As long ago as biblical times, predators and wilderness were viewed with hostile fervor. Wilderness is mentioned 245 times in the Old Testament and always as a godless environment. Predators in the Middle Ages—particularly wolves and bears—were accused of conscious viciousness. It was believed that the Devil dwelt in wolves, and so-called werewolves were put to death during the Inquisition.

The idea of The Evil Deceiver, the wolf, in the story of *Little Red Riding Hood* was very much in the minds of the early colonists. To those who left the tame and orderly fields and farms of Europe, the vast forests of the New World and their wild animals were terrifying. One early journal referred to this new country as a "hideous and desolate wilderness." Superstitions and myths abounded in these newcomers, to the astonishment of Native Americans who viewed all creatures as brothers and sisters. The early explorers Lewis and Clark described the grizzly bear as a "monstrous animal and a most terrible enemy." Much later, even the dedicated conservationist Theodore Roosevelt called the wolf "the beast of waste and desolation."

Such deeply held attitudes are part of our culture and, therefore, change slowly. Most people will still cheer for deer, rabbits, and squirrels that are being pursued. They admit that they hope coyotes, snakes, spiders, and hawks will fail.

The late wolf authority, Durward L. Allen, told of his mother's witnessing the killing of a dog by a coyote. "Why can't they be nice?" she asked.

But although predators possess instinctive skills in capturing and killing, prey have their own clever methods of hiding and avoiding capture. It is estimated, for example, that only one chase out of twelve ends in a substantial meal for a wolf and its pups. Predators and their young often go hungry. And, of course, because there is more food available for herbivores, there are many more prey animals than predators.

It would seem that our sympathies are misplaced. That's what makes studying predators so fascinating! And learning about nature's hunters can be especially appealing to children because these are real games and adventures. This is The Chase and Hide-and-Seek all rolled into one. The title *Everybody's Somebody's Lunch* is a fun way of describing life's food chain.

While this Teacher's Guide is directed toward grades three to six, there are differences in age and development to consider in presenting tooth-and-claw predator/prey relationships. Tread lightly. Some children will be more sensitive to the subject than others. But with gentle guidance and patience they should come to play the games and do the exercises suggested in the following pages and begin to feel comfortable with the idea of a fox eating a squirrel.

The activities and lessons that follow focus on the predators of North America and describe sample species in the categories of mammals, birds, reptiles, amphibians, invertebrates and fish. Also included is a rundown of places where wildlife and habitat are protected.

Finally, two important topics are offered for study that can stimulate lively and useful classroom discussions: the role of humans as predators and death in nature.

But this Guide is meant to be just a start. We hope our suggestions for projects will inspire you to expand on these themes in ways that suit the children you are teaching. As they come to appreciate the vital role that predatory wildlife plays in nature, misunderstanding will give way to awe. It's exciting to watch this happen.

Ideally, these new attitudes will be passed along to family and friends so that one day soon, predators will be treated with the compassion and respect they deserve as true wonders of a wild world we are in danger of losing. The greatest gift we can give predators is to understand them. In the words of the Senegalese poet, Babr Dioum Dioum:

> IN THE END, WE CONSERVE ONLY WHAT WE LOVE.
> WE LOVE ONLY WHAT WE UNDERSTAND.
> WE UNDERSTAND ONLY WHAT WE ARE TAUGHT.

—Cherie Mason
and Judy Kellogg Markowsky

"I'll have the cream of rabbit soup, the
baked-stuffed mouse, and for dessert,
raspberry-beetle pie."

WE VALUE THE INDIVIDUAL SUPREMELY,
AND NATURE VALUES HIM NOT A WHIT.
—*Annie Dillard*

CHAPTER ONE
What Do You Know about Predators?

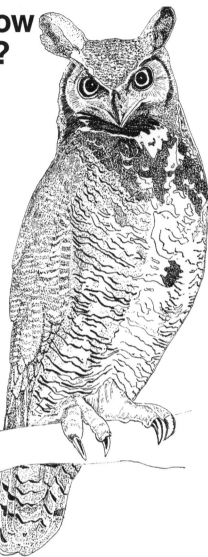

They act out of instinct, not out of meanness. That's why we shouldn't get angry with them when they kill other animals we like.

•Prey animals do not live lives of terror, expecting to be killed at any moment. They do try to escape from predators, but when the end is near, most prey animals go into shock and lose consciousness. Usually death comes quickly.

•Predators don't always catch their prey. Sometimes only one try in twelve is successful.

•Predators don't "wipe out" prey populations. There are always more prey animals than predators.

•Predators must surprise their prey to catch them and that isn't always easy.

•Often predators go hungry or settle for almost anything. If not a squirrel, then maybe a grasshopper or just a few berries or even animals already dead.

•Sometimes predators kill other predators (wolves will kill coyotes, shrews will kill snakes).

•Most predators are protective and attentive parents.

•Most of the offspring of predators die before adulthood.

•There are many unlikely predators: a robin, pulling out a worm; any warbler, snatching a caterpillar; a little salamander, crawling under leaves for insects; frogs and toads, flipping out their tongues for insects.

•With very few exceptions, North American predators don't attack and kill humans.

CHAPTER TWO
Some Definitions

Predator: *an animal that hunts other animals for food.*

Prey: *an animal that is killed by another animal for food.*

Carnivore: *an animal whose diet is mostly meat. Examples: wolf, owl.*

Herbivore: *an animal whose diet is plants. Examples: rabbit, deer.*

Omnivore: *an animal that eats both plants and animals. Examples: fox, bear.*

Insectivore: *an animal that eats insects. Examples: some bats, frogs.*

• Have students make lists of species that are carnivores, herbivores, omnivores, insectivores.

Who's Whose Lunch?

Objective: Children will learn which animals fit into the above categories. They will also learn there is overlap among the categories. Some animals are both predator and prey. Some eat mostly meat, but a little vegetable matter.

Concept: Brainstorming in class, children will assign familiar local wild animals to lists of the above categories.

You Will Need:
- *Pencil and paper*
- *Or large paper and easel*
- *Or writing board*

What to Do: Ask children what wild animals they have seen or know about.
Do they have a favorite?
Is their favorite a predator or prey?
Or sometimes both?

Who's whose lunch?

Amazing Misunderstood Animals

Not everyone appreciates animals like bats, snakes, and scorpions. Even those misunderstood animals are special, though. Each of the sentences below contains an extra letter—repeated many times—that does not belong.

• **Cross out the extra letter wherever it appears in the sentence. Then read the amazing fact about a misunderstood animal.**

1. Slome spliders clatch linsects by splitting lon thelm.

2. Dif somed shdarks stdop swidmming, thedy sdink.

3. Then noctopus hans a bneak liken a parront's.

4. Somer brats wreigh lerss tharn a prenny.

5. Koing snakooes omay eato ratoolesnakooes.

6. Ya moyther scyorpyion cyarries hyer byabies yon hery byack.

7. Farmadilloffs feat blafck widowf spfiders.

8. Sobmetibmes pirbanhabs beat frubit.

9. Wolvecs care gocod parcents. Thec mothcer cand facther worck togecther toc craise thecir pucps.

10. Skungks gwill spragy gonly tog protegct themseglvegs.

• **Choose one of the misunderstood animals above.**
• **Write what you like best about the animal you chose.**

Teacher: You may want to challenge students to read each silly sentence aloud and then read the correct sentence.

Text reprinted with permission from the National Association for Humane and Environmental Education, publishers of KIND News, P.O. Box 362, East Haddam, CT 06423-0362.

Text reprinted with permission from the National Association for Humane and Environmental Education, publishers of *KIND News*, P.O. Box 362, East Haddam, CT 06423-0362.

Know Your Predators

What do these animals have in common? They are all predators.
Predators eat other animals in order to live.

- **Use the words from the Word Box to answer the crossword clues.
  Cross off each word as you use it.**

Word Box

frog	barracuda	snake	robin	anemone
eagle	tiger	bat	raccoon	owl
wolf	spider	orca	shrew	ladybug

Across

2. This small, furry, mouselike predator injects victims with venom.
4. This flying mammal eats mosquitoes.
6. This reptile predator often helps farmers by eating mice.
10. This fish is a fierce ocean predator.
13. This bird is a symbol of the United States.
14. This bird flies at night and mostly eats mice and other rodents.
15. This predator is related to the dogs we keep as pets.

Down

1. This large mammal lives in the ocean and eats mostly seals.
3. This insect predator eats tiny insects that feed on garden plants.
5. This large predator's fur is striped.
7. This bird is known for a red breast and eats worms and insects.
8. This eight-legged predator is actually not an insect.
9. This amphibian eats many insects.
11. This predator often "washes" food before eating it.
12. This ocean predator cannot swim and waits for dinner to float by.

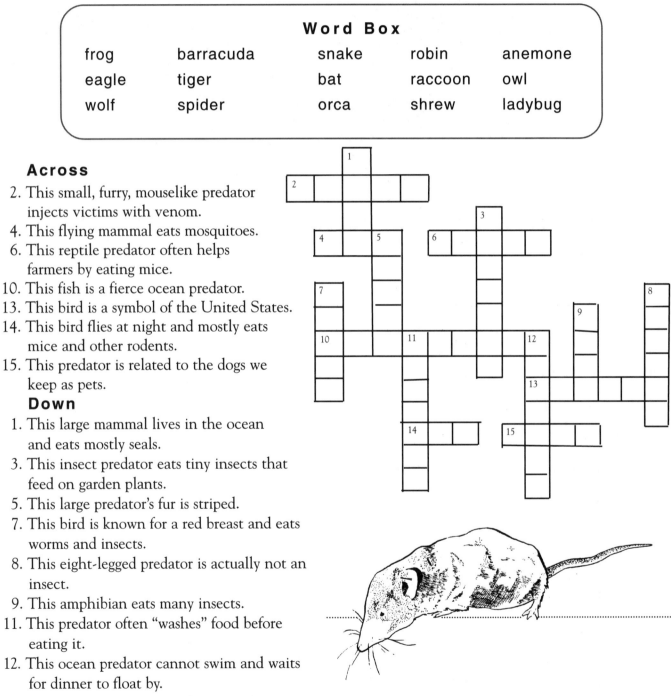

Teacher: Use this worksheet when teaching about endangered species.
Remind students that many predators are endangered and need our help.

Only to the white man was nature a wilderness
and only to him was the land "infested"
with "wild" animals and "savage" people.
To us it was tame.
Earth was bountiful and we were surrounded with the
blessings of the Great Mystery.

–Chief Luther Standing Bear of the Oglala Sioux

CHAPTER THREE
The Food Chain: Everybody IS Somebody's Lunch

SUN

A food chain is a way of describing who eats whom in an ecosystem.

These pictures are simplified symbols, or conceptual models. They show the natural role of predation in the redistribution and recycling of energy through plants and animals in an ecosystem.

The Food Chain
The food chain shows the links that bind an ecosystem together. Its first link is the sun, the source of energy that a plant uses to make its own food from air, water, and a few minerals. The next link in the food chain is a plant, then an herbivore which eats the plant, and then a carnivore, which eats the herbivore. Thus the sun's energy is captured by plants, and moves as food into the bodies of herbivores. This food then moves into the body of a predator when it kills and eats the herbivore.

P a p e r   C h a i n

Objective: To learn the links in a simple food chain.

Concept: Plants and animals are linked in a predator-prey relationship.

You Will Need:
- *Strips of construction paper*
- *Pictures of plants and animals*

What to Do: Children enjoy making paper chains with strips of construction paper. They will enjoy adding in the links of a simple food chain:
> 1) cut-outs of the *sun*
> 2) *green grass*
> 3) *a mouse*
> 4) *and a fox*

Or, they might prefer to choose their *own* favorite local animals. *Let them decide* how to attach their chain links together.

E c o l o g y   B l o c k s

Objective: To learn in a simplified way how species are interdependent.

Concept: An energy pyramid is like a food chain, but different in that *it symbolizes the relative amount of food needed to support herbivores & carnivores.* For example, it takes a lot of grass and grass seeds to feed mice. So plants are at the base of the pyramid. If you could weigh all the grass, it would weigh a lot more than all the mice.

Mice are herbivores, so they are in the narrower part of the pyramid above the grass. If you could imagine weighing all the mice together, they would weigh less than the grass, but more than the fox.

Predators need plants, too! Even though they may not eat the plants directly, the predator eats the animal that eats the plants, thereby depending on plants.

You Will Need:
- *Wooden blocks, all the same size*
A parent who enjoys carpentry would likely be happy to saw and sand some for you.

What to Do: Have the children research several species in a simplified food chain in your local ecosystem. Then they can draw illustrations of, or glue cut-outs of, these species onto wooden blocks. They'll need to do a little math. How many blocks should be on the bottom layer? These should represent herbivores. How many in the next layer? These could have a carnivore on top of them, at the top of the food chain.

Then children can build their pyramid, arranging the layers in order. Now comes the fun part. Why don't we want a species to become extinct? **Remove one of the blocks and see!**

Text reprinted with permission from the National Association for Humane & Environmental Education, publishers of KIND News, P.O. Box 362, East Haddam, CT 06423-0362.

Predator Puzzle

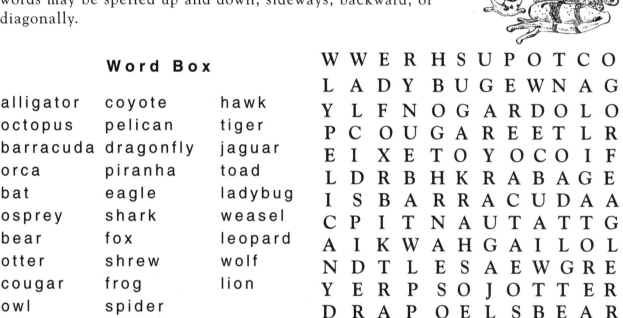

All of the animals below are predators. That means they eat other animals. Like all animals, predators are an important part of their habitats.

• Circle the names of the animals hidden in the puzzle. The words may be spelled up and down, sideways, backward, or diagonally.

Word Box

alligator	coyote	hawk
octopus	pelican	tiger
barracuda	dragonfly	jaguar
orca	piranha	toad
bat	eagle	ladybug
osprey	shark	weasel
bear	fox	leopard
otter	shrew	wolf
cougar	frog	lion
owl	spider	

```
W W E R H S U P O T C O
L A D Y B U G E W N A G
Y L F N O G A R D O L O
P C O U G A R E E T L R
E I X E T O Y O C O I F
L D R B H K R A B A G E
I S B A R R A C U D A A
C P I T N A U T A T T G
A I K W A H G A I L O L
N D T L E S A E W G R E
Y E R P S O J O T T E R
D R A P O E L S B E A R
```

When natural habitats are destroyed, animals lose their homes and food. What message do animals have for people?

• From left to right, read the uncircled letters in the puzzle. Write the message on the blank lines below:

_____ _____ _____

• Choose one of the animals from the puzzle. On the back, draw a picture of that animal in a natural habitat. Under your drawing write: "Predators need their habitats."

Teacher: Use this worksheet as a springboard for discussion about the important roles predators play in a balanced ecosystem.

IN NATURE, PREDATORS DO NOT NORMALLY EAT ALL THE PREY AND THEN GO EXTINCT.

ROBINS EAT WORMS, BUT EVERY YEAR THERE ARE STILL ROBINS AND WORMS.

–Paul Ehrlich

The Predacious Robin

Objective: Children will learn that a familiar bird, not seeming very fierce, is nevertheless a predator.

Concept: The familiar robin is at the top of a simple food chain or pyramid. It eats worms, which in turn eat decaying leaves.

You Will Need:
- *Cardboard*
- *Some dry leaves*
- *Some plastic worms**

What to Do: Children can draw, color, and cut out a life-sized robin from cardboard or heavy paper. The bill should be open. One end of the worm should be attached to the robin's bill, and the other end should go through a hole in a cardboard triangle.

Children will enjoy making their demonstration of predation dramatic, and they will enjoy being ingenious in attaching the worm. They can then glue a few worms below the robin, and a few dead leaves below the worms on the pyramid.

- The display, when finished, should also symbolize the "Food Pyramid."

Often used as a bait in fishing; sold in sporting goods stores. If plastic worms prove too expensive, brown string or brown construction paper "worms" could be substituted.

CHAPTER FOUR
Predator Tools–Formidable and Fascinating

Most hawks grab their prey with their powerful claws, called talons.

Teeth

A coyote killing a cat would likely run alongside the fleeing cat, grabbing it by the neck and shaking it. The coyote's teeth would puncture or sever the spinal cord, causing death quickly. This may have happened to Mouser the night before the story in *Everybody's Somebody's Lunch* begins.

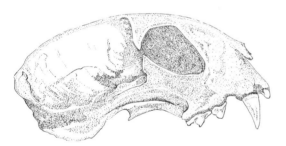

The bobcat's dagger-shaped canine teeth are used for piercing and stabbing.

Teeth and Claws Together

A bobcat killing a rabbit would pounce, grabbing prey with its teeth and claws and puncturing it with the long canine teeth.

More Claws, Called Talons

Most hawks grab their prey with their powerful claws, called talons. Hawks' feet crush and talons pierce, and if that's not enough, their sharp bill can rip flesh or snip through the neck. An osprey, often called a fish hawk, grabs a fish in the water with its talons and carries it to a tree branch. Then, with its sharp bill it rips the fish open, much like a person "cleaning" a fish.

More Teeth

Both the shrew and snake in the story are predators, and either one might eat the other! Both have sharp teeth to grab beetles, worms, slugs, and other small prey.

Fangs: Hollow Teeth that Inject Poison

The spider who caught the horsefly in its web would wrap its prey in spider silk, as well as bite it with its hollow fangs, injecting lethal venom. The venom would kill the horsefly as well as liquefy its internal organs. The spider would then suck out the liquid. Many children have watched this happen—ask your students if they have seen it. Other flies may have flown around the same web, or may have struggled free before the spider had a chance to bite.

Tongues–Soft but Catchy

The little tree frog in the story is a predator, too. It would wait quietly on a tree branch until an insect flew close by. Then it would flip out its sticky tongue, bringing the insect back into its mouth. A frog flips its tongue at many flies, but only catches some.

A hawk's sharp bill is often markedly hooked, and is used for plucking and tearing.

How Do Predators Use Their Tools to Get Their Lunch?

Death is dramatic and awe-inspiring. Children will find it motivating to research (and even write about) how their favorite predator catches and kills its prey.

Children can read natural history books about their favorite predator.

Often the book glosses over this aspect of an animal's life. If so, a person knowledgeable about wildlife can help explain it in a way that satisfies the children's curiosity.

How Can Prey Get Away?

Children will enjoy thinking about this question and coming up with their own answers. Ask them, "Did you ever see a mouse or a rabbit run? *Does their color help them?* What kinds of places can they hide?"

They will also enjoy reading about their favorite kind of prey animal. What *behavior* or *adaptations* will help it *escape* from a predator?

Your school library may have books about *animal camouflage*; children love to search the pictures for *hidden animals*.

Without Tools, the Prey Gets Away

Objective: Children will learn why predators need their "tools"—sharp teeth and claws.

Concept: Without sharp teeth or claws, the predator can't get lunch.

You Will Need: • *A cut-out shape of a mouse's face and ears*
• *A thick, soft mitten*

What to Do: Have two children demonstrate.
One child's hand is the mouse.
The other child wears the thick, soft mitten. This child's hand is a predator with no tools!
The hand comes down and tries to grab the mouse. The mouse tries to wiggle away. Of course, it's easy, because the predator has no tools!

CHAPTER FIVE
Predatory Mammals

Once the most persecuted of predators, wolves now have a growing number of supporters throughout the U.S.

How Bad Is the Big, Bad Wolf?

Although wolves have lived in America for two million years, they are still among our most misunderstood animals. When the Colonists came to America, they brought their superstitions and fears about the wolf with them. And when The Evil One of *Little Red Riding Hood* began to prey on their food animals, they began a war on the "varmints." Thus began a long history of persecution of wolves. They were trapped, poisoned, and shot down through the decades in a frenzy to wipe out the species. And it almost succeeded. But since the passage of the Endangered Species Act in 1973, the wolf has made a modest comeback. About 7,000 gray wolves still exist in Alaska; the species is not "endangered" there, so it is not protected from aerial hunting, trapping, and the paying of bounties or rewards for wolf pelts. But wolves have made a recovery in Minnesota and a few are gaining a foothold in Wisconsin, Michigan, and the northern Rocky Mountains where they are protected. They have also recolonized Glacier National Park and parts of Montana. Meantime, there is growing support for helping the wolf return to other parts of its native range.

In real life, wolves are not vicious killers, nor are they animals to be cross-bred with dogs and kept as pets. They are powerful, intelligent, social animals that live in highly organized packs which consist of a breeding pair and subordinate individuals. Wolf defenders are quick to point out that documented evidence of a wild wolf attacking and killing a human is virtually nonexistent.

Although its official common name is the gray wolf, there are different names for wolves in different parts of the country. In the eastern U.S. and Canada, forest-dwelling wolves are called timber wolves, in the Southwest, they're Mexican wolves, and in the far north, Arctic wolves. A separate rare species, the red wolf, is native to the Southeast.

The eastern timber wolf generally weighs fifty to eighty-five pounds; males are somewhat larger than females. The wolf is well-adapted to its role as a predator at the top of the food chain. Its long legs, keen sense of smell, and sharp canine teeth are the tools of a successful hunter. Under the right conditions, wolves can hear sounds up to six miles away. They can run as fast as forty miles per hour and can maintain that speed for twenty minutes in pursuing prey long distances. Most important, cooperation with their pack-family enables them to capture large animals like elk and moose.

However, evolution has "wised-up" prey species.

They have learned how to escape and certainly aren't "sitting ducks" whenever a wolf appears. It has been estimated that only one chase in twelve ends in a successful kill. Deer and moose can run swiftly and are capable of delivering deadly blows with hooves or antlers. Beaver escape into water. So wolves are not able to wipe out their prey. Yet they play an important role in natural ecosystems. For example, in studying the effects of reintroduced wolves to Yellowstone National Park, it has been observed that after only the first two years, they had killed or driven out half the coyotes in the area. With fewer coyotes, rodents became more plentiful, thus providing more food for other predators like hawks and bald eagles. Their effect on grizzly bears was even more remarkable. The bears prospered, thanks to the leftovers the wolves left behind, especially wolf-killed elk, which the bears feed on before their long winter sleep. These changes happened because a major predator returned to a large ecosystem.

One of the most distinctive features of wolves is their howling. As soon as one wolf starts to howl, the others in the pack join in. They have been observed to change the pitch of the howls, in what could be interpreted as an attempt to harmonize. Wolves separated from the pack signal their location with a short, mournful howl.

Let's all let out a loud wolf's howl for this symbol of untamed wilderness!

Do You Say "Coyote" or "Coyotee"?

This smaller cousin of the wolf is also widely feared and hated. The U.S. Government continues to trap and poison coyotes and other predators by the millions in its Animal Damage Control Program on federal lands in the West, where sheep and cattle graze. But the coyote is a survivor, a reason why the Navajos named him "God's Dog." With inherent intelligence and unfussy food habits, the little song-dog of the West has expanded its territory by exploring new places, sampling new food, and testing new dangers, so that now its numbers are so widespread that it even shows up in suburban backyards! Surely, the coyote is one of nature's greatest success stories.

Like wolves, coyotes use their keen sense of smell to locate prey. Like wolves, they are very vocal. A few yelps and barks followed by a long howl that ends with a few short yaps tells you that coyotes, not wolves, are serenading.

Coyotes often hunt alone at night and may travel for long distances in search of food. Weighing an average of only thirty-five to fifty pounds, depending on where they live, they sometimes hunt in pairs or packs to bring down large prey. They also steal the prey of other carnivores. A common trick is to wait at the end of a burrow and pounce on an animal as it flees from a pursuing predator. Rabbits and rodents are their main food. However, if necessary, they will eat birds' eggs, reptiles, insects, frogs, even fish, as well as fruits and garden vegetables. In short, like most predators they are opportunists; they must eat what they can find. In urban areas, cats and small dogs left outside become easy prey for coyotes. Did a coyote kill Mouser in *Everybody's Somebody's Lunch*? It's very possible.

These are smart, tough, wild animals!

The Little Foxes

Foxes are small canids with pointed muzzles, large ears, and long bushy tails. Several different species inhabit the U.S.: the endangered swift fox or kit fox; the gray fox, also called the tree fox because it can climb trees; and the most familiar, the red fox, probably the most adaptable of all carnivores. There is even a seldom-seen mountain fox called the "ghost fox," which is a special type of red fox found in the Rockies, the Cascades, and the Sierra Nevadas.

Foxes are killed by humans for four basic reasons: for sport; for predator control; for their pelts (fur); and for rabies control. Of the four, being trapped for their fur has had the most widespread effect on fox populations. Fortunately, like the coyote, foxes continue to survive.

All foxes are opportunistic hunters, which means they can quickly change their hunting technique from stealth to dash-and-grab. And they will eat almost anything that's available, from rodents to birds to grasshoppers to even earthworms. Anyone who has seen a fox gently pull an earthworm out of the ground will not soon forget it. Of course, unpenned domestic chickens and ducks are fair game anytime for foxes.

When in season, such fruit as strawberries, blackberries, and apples can account for most of a fox's diet. Nevertheless, foxes have some preferences. Red foxes prefer meadow voles above everything. However, they know enough to cache even unfavored prey for future use, and they seem to have a good memory for the location of these "pantries."

Red foxes catch rodents with their famous "mouse leap," springing as much as three feet off the ground and diving, front paws first, onto the prey.

People tend to like foxes. In fact, one of the highest compliments anyone can receive is to be told, "You're smart as a fox!

Wild Cats and House Cats: Powerful Predators

Cougar, puma, panther, and mountain lion: all names for the same animal! This is one of the largest native cats in North America. It can be six to seven feet long and weigh up to 280 pounds. Excessive hunting, trapping, and predator-control programs have greatly reduced its numbers. The Eastern cougar or panther is listed as an endangered species; there are presently only thirty to fifty remaining in Florida. All of the large cats have lost nearly two-thirds of their habitat and are thus coming into more contact with humans. Inexperienced juvenile cougars are especially dangerous, and there have been some attacks on people by these solitary predators. They usually seek out prey larger than themselves, such as deer and elk. Excellent climbers, they will often lie in wait in tree branches and leap on the prey's back, biting into the neck.

Lynx

The Canada lynx is rare in the Continental U.S. mainly because it has been heavily trapped. While there are thousands of lynxes in Canada and Alaska, only a few hundred are left in Maine, Montana, and Washington.

The lynx is an agile predator about three feet long and weighing up to 30 pounds. It's a strong swimmer and hunts mostly at night. Wide, furred feet enable the lynx to pursue its favorite food, the snowshoe hare, one of the few animals that can move through the snow faster than the lynx.

Ocelot

Only about a hundred ocelots still exist in the U.S., all of them in the southern part of Texas. About the size of a bobcat, the ocelot is an excellent climber and swimmer. Its prey is small mammals, birds and reptiles. Its enemies are people, coyotes, and wild dogs, which is why they prefer the densest underbrush, where they are almost impossible to see.

Bobcat

The bobcat is doing fairly well across North America, although its population has been greatly reduced. In fact, a few years ago it was being considered for the International Endangered and Threatened Species list. The bobcat is the feline jack-of-all trades. It will eat whatever happens to be abundant and available at the time, whether it's squirrels, rats, birds, snakes, lizards, or even insects. But like most cats, it lacks endurance and must get its prey in a few surprise strides or jumps. It is one of the few predators that can kill a porcupine. It does so by getting down low, under the face where there are no quills. The average "wildcat" weighs about twenty pounds and measures about three feet.

Claws of a wild cat

House Cat, the Predator that Lives with You

What does your pet cat do outdoors all day and night? In *Everybody's Somebody's Lunch* the story begins with the girl looking for her cat in the woods. Should her cat have been allowed to roam outside? What were the dangers for the cat and for the wildlife?

Americans keep an estimated 60 million cats as pets. Let's say that each cat kills only ONE bird a year. That would mean that cats kill a minimum of 60 million birds a year. Scientific studies actually show that each year cats kill HUNDREDS OF MILLIONS of migratory songbirds. In 1990 researchers estimated that "outdoor" house cats and feral cats were responsible for killing nearly 78 million small mammals and birds annually in the United Kingdom. Dr. Stanley Temple at the University of Wisconsin estimates that 20 to 150 million songbirds are killed each year by rural cats in that state alone.

Feline predation is NOT "natural." Cats were domesticated by the ancient Egyptians and taken throughout the world by the Romans. They were brought to North America to control rats. The pussycat that sits curled up on your couch is not a natural predator and has never been in the natural food chain in the western hemisphere.

Cats are a serious threat to fledglings, birds roosting at night, and birds on a nest. Research shows that declawing and attaching bells to collars are futile. Clawless cats still wield lethal teeth, and any cat worth its catnip can stalk without ringing a bell.

And at what risk are the cats? They can get lost, stolen, die from the cold, diseases, attacks from other animals, or be run over. An outdoor cat has a much shorter life than one that lives indoors. So how much of a favor are you doing your much-loved cat by letting it spend its life outdoors? Better to give it toys, a companion cat, and a window seat to curl up on. Better still, give your cat more play and grooming time with you!

The Grizzly Bear vs. the Shrew-- Which Is Fiercer?

Grizzly Facts

The grizzly is the largest of the land carnivores and is usually found only in wilderness areas. Those in Alaska (the Kodiak or brown bear) can reach eight feet in length and weigh as much as 1,700 pounds. They move at speeds of up to twenty miles an hour.

> MANY TIMES I HAVE LOOKED INTO THE EYES OF WILD ANIMALS, AND WE HAVE PARTED FRIENDS.
>
> *—Grace Seton Thompson*

The powerful claws of a grizzly are four inches long enabling the bear to dig for much of its food. Although classified as carnivores, grizzly bears relish roots and grasses. But they can also bring down a deer, elk, or smaller animals such as gophers and rodents. As wild salmon swim upstream to spawn, these giant bears feast for days, fattening up for the winter. Grizzlies got their name from the white-tipped, "grizzled" hair of their coats.

Shrew Facts

There are many different species of shrews. A shrew must eat constantly, consuming more than half its own weight every day in earthworms, insects, small mice, spiders, songbirds, and other shrews. The short-tailed shrew is the size of one's thumb, and is thought to be the only North American mammal with a venomous bite. It has been known to kill a three-pound rabbit and, as described in *Everybody's Somebody's Lunch*, it isn't unusual for a tiny shrew to take on a seven-inch ring-necked snake. Shrews make tasty snacks for owls and hawks, but four-legged predators seldom eat the feisty little critters because of their unpleasant odor. However, the weasel doesn't seem to mind the smell of its lunch!

So, is the grizzly bear fiercer, or the shrew? What's YOUR answer?

Bats in Your Belfry? Congratulations!

A single little brown bat can catch 600 mosquitoes in just one hour! Important agricultural plants—from bananas and mangoes to cashews, dates, and figs—rely on bats for pollination and seed dispersal.

Bats are the only mammals capable of true flight! They are not blind, and they do not become entangled in human hair. They have an excellent sense of sight and smell, but that's not how they catch their prey. Because they are nocturnal, they find their prey through the magic of echolocation. What that means is a bat emits high-pitched, sonar-like clicks that make it possible for it to both detect the wind sounds of flying insects and fly in total darkness without bumping into anything. But, believe it or not, some insects are clever enough to escape. For example, a certain moth can imitate those ultrasound clicks and while the confused bat is off on a wild goose chase, the moth gets away! One of the best ways to remain uneaten is simply to stay very still. Some nocturnal insects move back into daylight. And others, like lacewings and praying mantises, have evolved a new way of hearing the calls of hunting bats. Their ears are literally bat detectors!

Bats seldom transmit disease to other animals or humans. All mammals can contract rabies. However, even the less than 1 percent of bats that do, normally bite only in self-defense, and pose little threat to people who do not handle them.

The bumblebee bat of Thailand weighs less than a penny, while giant flying foxes of Indonesia have wingspans of up to six feet! The common little brown bat of North America is the world's longest-lived land mammal for its size, with life spans sometimes exceeding thirty-two years!

Compare Two Predators

Objective: To utilize a systematic method of comparison; to learn how predator roles differ.

Concept: Predators have different sizes, ranges, habitats, and behavior. These differences mean that predator species, even though they may seem similar, will take different prey species.

You Will Need: • *Research and writing skills*

What to Do: Children will make a table for two similar species they wish to compare:

Predator	Predator
Size	Size
Range	Range
Habitat	Habitat
Method of killing prey	Method of killing prey
Usual prey species	Usual prey species
Other relevant behavior	Other relevant behavior

• Just for contrast, try comparing a **grizzly bear** to a **shrew!**

Which is fiercer?

Mousy Math and the Role of Predators

Objective: To demonstrate how prolific prey species can be.

Concept: Most prey species have many, many young. What would happen if there were no predators? This math is simplified, but useful to demonstrate the concept with children.

You Will Need: • *Pencil, paper, or computer*

What to Do: Ask children to create a poster of how mice would reproduce in the absence of predators. Suppose a mouse had four young every two months all year. Let your students do the math and create the mice.

January-February	*1 mouse*
March-April	*4 mice!*
May-June	*16 mice!*
July-August	*64 mice!*
September-October	*256 mice!*
November-December	*1,024 mice!!*

Coyote Math

Objective: To use math to understand a coyote's diet.

Concept: Math is important for scientists. It helps them understand the importance of predators. A scientist studying coyotes found a coyote that was killed by a car halfway through the day. She cut open its stomach to see what it had eaten that day, and found nine voles (a vole is a kind of mouse with a short tail and small ears).

You Will Need: • *Pencil, paper*

What to Do: Ask the children to figure out, based on the above experience, how many *voles* a coyote might eat in a whole day, in a week, and in a month.

• Ask the children if they think this method might work for a *whole year.**

***Note:** Chances are this would not give a complete picture of a coyote's diet. Any predator's diet is likely to change with the seasons, and with prey availability. How could a scientist gain a full understanding of what prey species coyotes eat? Some scientists study the stomach contents of coyotes killed throughout the year; some scientists analyze coyote "scat" (feces).

Adapted from the "Coyote Kit" with permission from the British Columbia Society for the Prevention of Cruelty to Animals, Vancouver, B.C. V6CIV5

Text reprinted with permission from the National Association for Humane & Environmental Education, publishers of KIND News, P.O. Box 362, East Haddam, CT 06423-0362.

The Coyote– Awful or Awesome?

• Circle the facts that are new to you.

Coyotes' main
foods are rabbits,
rodents, and dead animals.
They also eat reptiles, birds,
fish, insects, and fruit.
Coyotes love
watermelon!

Coyotes
are very curious
and
intelligent.

Most coyotes
weigh less than thirty-
five pounds. They are
about four feet long from
the tips of their noses to
the tips of their tails.

Coyotes
may travel fifty
miles in a night,
hunting for
food.

A
coyote can
leap fourteen
feet!

Coyotes are
excellent parents.
They often live in
family groups. There
may be ten pups in
a litter.

A coyote
can jump over a
fence that is four
feet high.

One coyote
will sometimes
bring food to
another who is
sick or hurt.

In
the desert, a
coyote can smell
water three feet
underground and dig a
"well" so that she or
he can drink.

Coyotes
can hear, see,
and smell very
well.

• Write your favorite coyote fact. Draw a picture to illustrate it.

Teacher: Use this page to help students learn about and appreciate this
misunderstood animal.

19

Bats in Your Hair—Not!

Objective: Children will learn the difference between folklore and scientific information about bats.

Concept: Bats are so wonderfully interesting, your children will love reading about them and checking out Web pages. Because bats are nocturnal, mysterious, and sometimes frightening to people, there is much folklore.

You Will Need: • *An easel or blackboard*

What to Do: Make two columns, labeling one column "Folklore" and the other one "Fact." Ask children what they have heard about bats. Put the children to work researching bats. Have them enter their findings in the appropriate column. How might the folklore hurt bats? What can be done to counteract it?

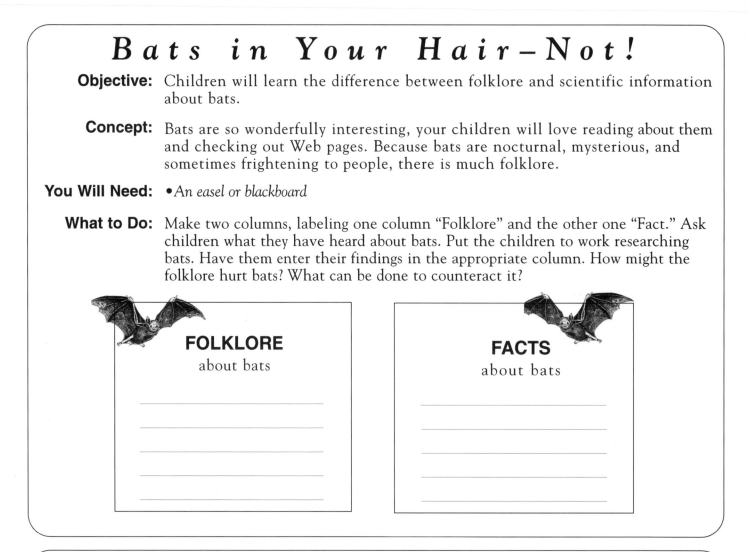

FOLKLORE
about bats

_____

_____

_____

_____

FACTS
about bats

_____

_____

_____

_____

_____

Bat and Moth in the Dark

Objective: Children will learn how bats find their way by echolocation.

Concept: How do bats avoid crashing into trees at night? They use echolocation, making tiny high-frequency noises that echo from twigs, trees, and even moths. This gives a bat a "sound picture" of its world that it interprets through those big ears.

You Will Need: • *Make a "bat cape" with cloth or paper wings, and wrist loops.*
You can make a crude one very simply, or a creative parent who likes to sew might enjoy making a well-sewn one for the class. Children will love wearing it. To play this group game, have children form a circle, holding hands. Explain to them that bats are *very* good listeners. Children also *must* be good listeners, very quiet and very considerate of their classmates, for this game.

What to Do: One child is chosen to be the bat and wear the cape and a blindfold. Two more children can be moths. It's fun and atmospheric for all the children if you can darken the room for this game. The bat wants to find moths in the dark, so the bat says softly, "Moth." Each moth-child then has to say softly, "Moth." The bat-child tries to find and touch a moth, using hearing only. Children must all be very quiet so the bat can hear. When the bat touches a moth, that moth joins the circle, and when both moths are found, three new children can be the bat and moths.

The Fox's Ears

Objective: To learn one way that a fox or coyote catches its prey.

Concept: Foxes and coyotes have very keen hearing. Their large ears catch and funnel sounds into the ear opening. They can hear a mouse squeaking or moving under grass, and under snow as well. A fox or a coyote will listen carefully while hunting in a field. When it hears a mouse, it will approach quietly, pinpoint the prey's location with its acute hearing, and sometimes make a prodigious leap, pinning the mouse to the ground with its front paws, then gobbling it up.

You Will Need: •*Nothing, really; but a picture of a fox and/or coyote face would be helpful.*

What to Do: Tell the children, dramatically, how a fox catches its prey, then ask them to demonstrate how the fox's big ears help it catch the mouse. Ask them to listen carefully while you make squeaking noises like a mouse.

Then ask them to cup their hands behind their ears, effectively enlarging their ears, making them big like those of a fox. Then you squeak again at the same volume.

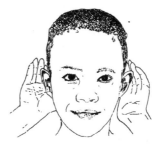

Can the children hear a difference? Why?

CHAPTER SIX
Predators with Wings

Eagles, hawks, falcons, owls and also, songbirds;
the great blue heron, cormorants, and even hummingbirds!

Owl's feathers are different from those of other birds. They are soft and velvety, with fringed edges that allow the owl to fly in silence, so the mouse doesn't hear it coming.

Beautiful, Noble, Fierce

Most people realize that birds of prey such as eagles, hawks and falcons are predators. Many people admire their fierceness, their wildness, their strength. You have probably seen advertisements that capitalize on noble images of hawks and eagles, symbols of wildness and freedom. TV footage of beautiful soaring hawks and eagles is used to sell cars! But birds of prey, also called raptors, have been severely persecuted by people, too.

Once Shot on Sight,
Now the Birdwatcher's Delight

Hawks were formerly shot by the thousands because they were thought to be killers of livestock such as chickens and lambs. Raptor numbers were seriously depleted by shooting. Some species, their numbers already depleted by shooting, became endangered because the use of the pesticide DDT interfered with their reproduction. Since the early 1970s, the use of DDT has been banned in the U.S.

> GIVE YOUR HEART TO THE HAWKS.
> *–Robinson Jeffers, poet and admirer of raptors*

But even now, although many people have learned the value of raptors like hawks and eagles, they are still shot and poisoned in ignorance, or in defiance of the law. Sometimes the bodies of hawks are strung up on fences, to defy the protective laws and to "teach a lesson" to other hawks.

Some hawks migrate south to other countries, where the use of DDT is still legal, so some hawks and falcons still accumulate DDT in their bodies.

Eagles are sometimes shot or poisoned because they are thought to prey on livestock. Their role as predators has been greatly misunderstood.

Birds of Prey, Seen by Day

We have two kinds of eagles in the U.S., the bald eagle and the golden eagle.

The bald eagle lives mostly along rivers, lakes, and the ocean and eats mostly fish. The golden eagle lives in upland areas (mountains and deserts) and eats mostly rabbits and rodents.

Birds of prey have adaptations and feeding styles that will fascinate children. Three kinds of raptors found nationwide will illustrate differences among the different kinds.

The *red-tailed hawk* is a soaring kind of hawk. It will soar in circles, or sit on a perch watching for rodents. Spotting a rat, it will drop down and grab it with its talons.

The *peregrine falcon* is a much faster bird. Not only a fast flyer, it can fold its wings in a controlled, well-aimed dive at nearly 200 miles per hour, its talons hitting a flying bird with great force. The prey bird is killed instantly, falling like a stone out of the sky.

Sometimes, instead of diving and striking, the peregrine falcon flies after its prey, grabbing it out of the air. Then, the falcon severs its prey's spinal cord. Falcons even have a special "tomial tooth" on the bill that helps do this.

The *sharp-shinned hawk* preys on other birds,

Robins are predators, too; they eat many insects as well as earthworms.

too. But its feeding style is quite different from that of the falcon. Relying on surprise, it hides in a tree and flies after small birds with a quick burst of speed. It twists and turns, chasing its prey among trees and grabbing with its talons.

Silent in Flight, Seen at Night

Hawks and eagles hunt in the day, while owls hunt mostly at night. Books about owls usually emphasize their eyes and ears, adapted for night hunting. Their ears are not symmetrical—one is higher, the other lower; one larger and differently shaped from the other. This helps the owl hear its prey (typically a mouse) slightly differently with each ear.

That helps the owl locate the mouse precisely in the dark. Owls' feathers are also different from those of other birds. They are soft and velvety, with fringed edges. The soft fringe helps the owl fly in silence, so the mouse doesn't hear it coming.

The red-tailed hawk soars in wide circles high in the sky, likely hunting for rodents in the meadows below. It will also sit motionless on a dead branch for hours at a time in wait for its lunch.

Little Songbirds—Also Predators with Wings— Kill Worms and Bugs and Other Things

The robin eating a worm, the chickadee eating an insect, the warbler eating a caterpillar are all predators as surely as the hawk is. Their bills are used to grasp and crush prey.

Herons are predators, too. Fish are their prey. Cormorants, because they are fish-eaters, are predators, too. Fish-eating birds are not appreciated, and sometimes are illegally shot, by people who want to raise or catch the same fish that the birds eat.

Crows are often predators, eating frogs, mice and smaller birds, although they also eat fruit and grain.

Even the tiny, beautiful hummingbird will snap up small insects as it visits flowers for their nectar.

Great Blue Heron Fish Toss

Objective: To learn that a great blue heron is a predator, and that it frequently misses its prey.

Concept: A fish-eater is a predator. The great blue heron, a well-known bird, catches and eats fish with its long bill, waiting patiently for a fish to come close rather than chasing it. Then it strikes, grabbing the fish in its bill rather than spearing it. Like any predator, the heron misses a large percentage of the time.

You Will Need:
- *Large, safe (not sharp) tongs shaped somewhat like a bird's bill*
- *A simulated fish (rubber fish are often sold in toy stores)**
- *A pail of water*

What to Do: Ask children if they have seen a great blue heron—a large, visually prominent and well-known bird. Ask a child to demonstrate how the heron catches a fish.

(**Note:** You need to stress good behavior and safety; children do get excited in this entertaining demonstration. The tongs must not have sharp edges or corners.)

The fish can start out **on the floor.** If children can easily pick up the fish from the floor with the tongs, add to the challenge by putting the rubber fish **in a pail of water**, making it more slippery.

Then you could **add a little mud** to the water, making it harder to see the fish, or you could put **simulated water plants** (paper strips or grass would do) in the pail, making it easier for the fish to hide.

Another challenge is to ask the children to **toss the fish** gently up in the air with the tongs and catch it again, as herons occasionally do with a large fish to ensure they swallow it headfirst. Children will enjoy this game a lot, and learn that it's not easy to be a predator.

*You want a heavy rubber fish that will *sink*, not float, in water.

25

Compare Two Predators

You did this already with predator mammals;
now why not try predators with wings?

Objective: To compare in a systematic way; to learn how predator roles differ.

Concept: Predators have different sizes, ranges, habitats and behavior. These differences mean that predator species, even though they may seem similar, will take different prey species.

You Will Need: • *Research and writing skills*

What to Do: Children will make a table for two similar species they wish to compare:

Predator	Predator
Size	Size
Range	Range
Habitat	Habitat
Method of Killing Prey	Method of Killing Prey
Usual Prey Species	Usual Prey Species
Other Relevant Behavior	Other Relevant Behavior

Make a Wingspan

Objective: Students will learn the size of bird wingspans, relevant to their own arm spans. In doing so, they will utilize measurement skills.

Concept: Birds of prey have large wingspans!

You Will Need: • *A roll of shelf paper*
• *Writing implements (crayons, markers)*
• *Scissors*

What to Do: Each student can draw and cut out a life-size wingspan of a favorite raptor. In some field guides to the birds, children can find the wingspans of most birds. For example, they will find that an eagle's wingspan is well over six feet, while that of a great blue heron is over five feet, that of an osprey is under five feet, the wingspan of a red-tailed hawk is about four feet, and the wingspan of a peregrine falcon is under four feet. Children will draw and cut out wingspan shapes the same length, size and shape as the wingspan of a selected bird. Some children will enjoy drawing feather patterns and coloring the wings to represent their selected bird. On the wingspans, they can write some of the habitat requirements and food of their predator with wings. They will enjoy comparing their own "arm span" to the bird's wingspans, and displaying the wingspans in the classroom.

CHAPTER SEVEN

Predators with Scales and Fins, Jointed Legs, and Slippery Skins

Wolves and shrews, hawks and songbirds are predators— and so are snakes, frogs, fish and insects!

Snakes

Why do people hate snakes so? It seems to be a spontaneous, knee-jerk reaction. However, snakes represent an important educational opportunity.

Children should know how to identify local venomous snakes. Be sure to tell them about their habits and how to avoid them. This is important safety knowledge.

The venom and fangs of poisonous snakes have really evolved to subdue prey, not to terrorize people. A rattlesnake will sometimes lie in wait on one end of a log, knowing that rats often use logs as runways. A rattlesnake has pits below its eyes that detect the heat of its warm-blooded prey. When it detects prey, it strikes. A rat bitten by a rattlesnake will try to hop away, but it won't get far. Soon it will collapse; the snake, following its trail, will soon find the rat and swallow it whole.

Many people loathe snakes, but your class is sure to have some children who are fascinated by them, and will love researching, reading, and yes, even writing about them. Children should also be encouraged to leave snakes alone, and not provoke or taunt them.

Turtles

Many aquatic turtles, even those that seem slow and small, are also predators. Your children may enjoy researching how something that seems so slow could catch its prey! Just to make it confusing, many land tortoises are herbivores.

Crocodiles and alligators are certainly predators— just look at those sharp, conical teeth. They have fascinating ways of catching their prey, too, which children will love reading and even writing about!

Many children are familiar with lizards. They may have seen anoles (a small lizard) or iguanas as pets. It may surprise your children to learn that the small anoles are more predacious than the larger iguanas.

Frogs, with their nearly human-like shapes and their wide smiles, are appealing. Frogs are also predators of insects, worms, and other animals that are small enough for a frog to catch with its sticky tongue or grab in its wide mouth. Large frogs and toads can even catch birds!

Salamanders

If you live in a forested area, your students may be familiar with salamanders found under decaying logs in the forest. Salamanders are amphibians, as frogs are. Amphibians have moist, thin skin that unfortunately does not protect them from pollution; hence their numbers are declining worldwide. Salamanders are predators of the many insects and worms found under leaves and logs of the forest floor. They make a quick lunge toward their prey and, if successful, grab it in their mouth.

Lizards and Salamanders– What's the Difference?

Many children (and adults, too) get salamanders and lizards confused. It is a good educational opportunity to straighten this out! Lizards are reptiles, with dry scaly skin, while salamanders are amphibians, having

27

(like frogs) smooth, wet, slippery skin without scales. Their similar shape causes the confusion. They also have another interesting similarity.

Lizards and salamanders are not only predators; they are often prey. Larger lizards, snakes, birds, and mammals eat them. But both lizards and salamanders have a trick that sometimes prevents their becoming somebody's lunch! If an attacking predator grabs the tail, it is detachable, and once detached, the tail thrashes and writhes convincingly on the ground, decoying the predator from its intended—and escaping—prey.

Fish are Predators, Too

Most fish are predators, eating fish smaller than themselves, or sometimes dining on shrimp or other animals in their aquatic habitat. Fish have wonderful adaptations as prey and predator.

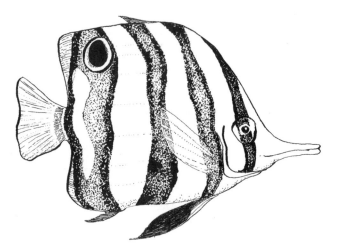

The butterfly fish's eyespot attracts predators away from the fish's vital area and thereby increases its chance of escape.

Some prey fish have a big eye-spot at the base of their tail. This has a very interesting function. A predator learns to aim just ahead of its prey, anticipating an attempt at escape. The eye-spot causes a predator to aim just behind, not in front of its prey. So the smaller fish dashes off, in exactly the opposite direction anticipated! No lunch!

The angler fish has a catchy way to get its prey. The fin on its back has a fleshy, wiggly, worm-like tip which lures in a smaller fish. Then, GULP! Lunch!

The archer fish has another neat trick. It spots an insect on a leaf above the water. With its mouth and tongue, it aims and squirts water at its prey, knocking it down onto the water's surface. Then, GULP! Lunch!

What's the best way to swallow a Stickelback? Certainly not tail-first. Note the sharp, strong spines along the ridge of its back, which can rip open the throat or stomach of its captor. This fearless little fish is scarcely over one inch long when fully grown!

Insects

The insect world is full of predators, too. Dragonflies eat smaller insects like mosquitoes. The praying mantis preys on many kinds of insects, and has even been photographed catching a hummingbird.

Everybody really IS somebody's lunch! The familiar, innocuous-looking ladybug is a predator of aphids, small herbivorous insects that suck plant juices.

Spiders Are Not Insects

Spiders are predators, and many children have observed them catching insects in their webs as described in *Everybody's Somebody's Lunch*. Ask your students if they have seen this phenomenon! People have a curious ambivalence about spiders; your students may be familiar with the much-loved Charlotte, the wonderful spider in E. B. White's book, *Charlotte's Web*. But most people abhor spiders in their homes, squashing them underfoot remorselessly.

Most spiders don't bite people, but if you live in an area where there are dangerous spiders, such as the black widow spider, or the brown recluse spider, it is valuable safety knowledge to know what these look like. Children knowledgeable about spiders are more likely to be respectful of all spiders, and to avoid the more dangerous ones for their own safety.

Daddy-longlegs (also called harvestmen) are related to spiders, but have differences, too. Some of the 3,000 daddy-longlegs species are predators, but they generally eat more vegetable matter than spiders do.

Scorpions are also predators. They are related to spiders and insects, and also can be dangerous to people. This represents another good opportunity for a combination of science and safety information.

These smaller predators, such as insects and spiders, are all around us, even in vacant lots and city homes, offering wonderful opportunities for young scientists to observe them in action.

Spiders Spin, Bite, Inject, and Suck: Watch a Spider in Action

Objective: To observe a spider systematically and with understanding.

Concept: Inside a dark garage or shed, often there will be a spider web against the windows. Why is that a good place for the spider to catch food? Children can look carefully for the spider, which often hides to one side of the web. If the web is a funnel-type web, the spider will be hiding in the narrow tube at the end of the funnel. When an insect lands in the web, the spider will dash out and capture the insect, bringing it back into the funnel to suck out its juices at leisure. Afterwards, the spider will remove victims from the web, dropping them below. How many can your children find?

You Will Need:
- *Pencil*
- *Paper*
- *Clipboard*

Spider in funnel web

What to Do: Children can use this form to collect data on the spiders they find:

Kind of Web:	Orb	☐
	Funnel	☐
	Basket	☐
	Bell-shaped	☐
	Other	☐
Location of Web:		
Location of Spider Relative to Web:		
# of Live Insects in Web:		
# of Dead Insects in Web:		
# of Dead Insects below Web:		

Children can use their data to answer questions:
What kind of web did they find most?
What kind of web, or location, caught the most insects?

Spider vs. Insect: What's the Difference?

Objective: Children will learn to differentiate spiders from insects.

Concept: Spiders and insects are both "arthropods"—jointed-legged animals—but it's easy to tell them apart. Spiders have eight legs, and their head and thorax (chest) are fused together. Insects have six legs, and their head and thorax (chest) are separated by a narrow neck.

You Will Need:
• *Paper and pencil*
• *Or, marker*

What to Do: Explain the difference between a spider and an insect. It's easy for you to make a simplified drawing of the two on a writing board, for children to compare. Tell children they will be scientific illustrators, drawing the difference between spiders and insects for a classmate. Have each child draw four insects and four spiders, randomly on a page. Then ask children to exchange drawings, and label each arthropod drawn as "Insect" or "Spider."

IMPARTIAL SYMPATHY TOWARD ALL CREATURES, REGARDLESS OF THEIR DIET,
IS AN ATTITUDE OF THE CULTIVATED MIND.   –*Durward L. Allen*

Spider vs. Insect: Which Is Which?

Objective: Children will learn to differentiate spiders from insects.

Concept: Spiders and insects are both "arthropods"—jointed-legged animals—but it's easy to tell them apart. Spiders have eight legs, and their head and thorax (chest) are fused together. Insects have six legs, and their head and thorax (chest) are separated by a narrow neck.

You Will Need:
• *A handful of plastic spiders and insects*
• *Two containers (to sort them into)*

What to Do: At Halloween time, buy several sets of mixed plastic insects and spiders. They are usually available in toy stores at that season. Put the spiders and insects in a jumble and ask children to separate them into two categories—"Insect" and "Spider"—based on the characteristics you have taught them. If the plastic insects are small, children will enjoy using tweezers to sort them, just as real entomologists do.

Teacher: Here are two different approaches to teach the same concept.

What's the Difference?

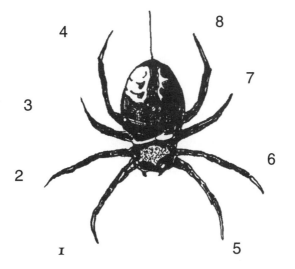

•A spider's head and thorax are fused and this structure is connected to the abdomen.

•A spider has eight legs.

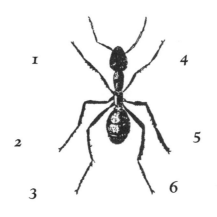

•The body of an insect is divided into a clearly defined head, thorax, and abdomen.

•An insect has 6 legs.

The Spider—
Awful or Awesome?

•Circle the facts that are new to you.

If
a spider loses a
leg, another will
grow in its place.

A
spider's legs are
attached to the
front part of its body.

Some spiders
live twenty or
thirty years.

Some spiders
can change
color.

The weight of
all the insects caught
by spiders every year is
equal to the weight of all
the people in the world.

A
spider's body is
divided into two parts.
(Insects' bodies have
three parts.)

Most
spiders have
eight eyes. Some
spiders who live in
caves don't have any
eyes.

Some spiders
live underwater in
bubbles trapped by
webs they have
made.

Not all spiders
make webs. Some
run and jump on
insects. Others catch
fish and birds to eat.

•Write your favorite spider fact. Then draw a picture to illustrate it.

Text reprinted with permission from the National Association for Humane and Environmental Education, publishers of *KIND News*, P.O. Box 362, East Haddam, CT 06423-0362.

Text reprinted with permission from the National Association for Humane and Environmental Education, publishers of *KIND News*, P.O. Box 362, East Haddam, CT 06423-0362

The Snake: Awful or Awesome?

•Circle the facts that are new to you.

Some snakes are only a few inches long. Others may be 30 feet long.

Snakes cannot close their eyes. Snakes' eyes are covered with a thin, clear scale.

A snake's tail is not poisonous. Most snakes have only one lung.

The tongue of a snake is soft. It is never used as a stinger.

Some snakes hatch from eggs. Others are born "ready to go."

Many snakes are great swimmers.

Snakes cannot see or hear well. One way they find out what is happening around them is by tasting the air with their tongues. This helps them find food and avoid enemies.

There are many more nonpoisonous snakes than poisonous ones.

Snakes are not slimy. They feel clean and smooth, like plastic.

Snakes can swallow things bigger than their heads.

•**Write a poem about a snake. Make your poem at least four lines long.**

Teacher: Use this page to help students learn about and appreciate this misunderstood animal.

Text reprinted with permission from the National Association for Humane and Environmental Education, publishers of *KIND News*, P.O. Box 362, East Haddam, CT 06423-0362.

The Scorpion— Awful or Awsome?

•**Circle the facts that are new to you.**

Baby scorpions spend the first week of their lives riding on their mother's back.

The hairs on a scorpion's legs can sense the movement of an insect two feet away.

Although they have eight eyes, scorpions can barely see.

Scorpions like to live in hot desert areas. They hide under rocks and logs in the daytime.

A scorpion can live for a year without eating.

Only a few of the 650 kinds of scorpions are deadly. Scorpions do not sting unless they are hurt, attacked, or frightened.

A scorpion's tail can wave in all directions.

At night scorpions come out to hunt. They grab insects and spiders with their pincers.

Male and female scorpions sometimes "dance," holding each other's pincers.

Some scorpions are only one quarter of an inch long. Others are eight inches long.

Roadrunners, owls, chickens, lizards, and chimpanzees eat scorpions.

•**Write a letter to a friend, telling why scorpions are awesome.**

Teacher: Use this page to help students learn about and appreciate this misunderstood animal.

A Lizard's Tale

Objective: Children will learn how some lizards and salamanders escape predation by losing their tail.

Concept: Lizards and salamanders have a trick which sometimes prevents their becoming somebody's lunch! If an attacking predator grabs the tail, the tail detaches, thrashing and writhing convincingly on the ground. The thrashing tail grabs the attention of the predator—the predator grabs the tail—meanwhile the lizard or salamander dashes away!

You Will Need: •Construction paper

What to Do: Have children cut out many lizard shapes by folding paper and cutting like this, with a constriction at the base of the tail:

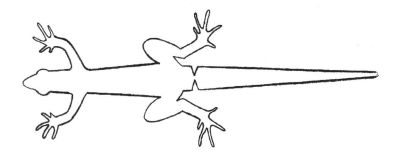

Then, they play a game in pairs:

One child moves the paper lizard along the desktop.
The other child—the "predator"—quickly puts a finger down on the moving lizard's tail.

What happens?

A Lizard's "Tale"

for cut-out

Some lizards and salamanders have developed a technique of releasing their tails to escape predation. Most lizards regrow their tails in a month; longer lizards take a year.

S n a k e S e n s e

Snakes live in almost all parts of the world, including hot deserts, cool forests, salty oceans, and warm, tropical seas. Like people, snakes need food, water, warmth, shade, and a clean, safe environment. How much do you know about snakes?

• **Answer the following questions by writing YES or NO in the blanks.**

1. Since all snakes are cold-blooded, does t<u>h</u>at mean their blood is always cold? _____
2. Do snakes live at the North and South pol<u>e</u>s? _____
3. A<u>r</u>e many snakes helpful to humans? _____
4. Do most snakes have a deadly <u>p</u>oison, called venom? _____
5. Do snakes' <u>e</u>yes ever close? _____
6. Do snakes ever ea<u>t</u> other snakes? _____
7. Do snakes chew their fo<u>o</u>d? _____
8. Do snakes smel<u>l</u> with their tongues? _____
9. Is the temperature inside a snake's b<u>o</u>dy the same as the temperature of the snake's environment? _____
10 When snakes hiss, rattle, bite, puff out, or play dead, are they tryin<u>g</u> to protect themselves from enemies? _____
11. Do snakes dr<u>i</u>nk water? _____
12. Can most snakes <u>s</u>wim? _____
13. Do snakes some<u>t</u>imes yawn? _____

> *How well did you do? Check your answers!*
>
> • Questions with an even number of words should be answered YES.
> • Questions with an odd number of words should be answered NO.

Each question above has an underlined letter.
• **In order, write down the underlined letters to finish this sentence:**
  A scientist who studies snakes is called a _ _ _ _ _ _ _ _ _ _ _ _ _.

Pretend you are a scientist who studies a certain kind of animal.
• **What animal would you study?**
• **What would you want to know about the animal?**
• **Write five questions about the animal. Use your library to research the answers.**

Teacher: Use this worksheet to encourage student's appreciation of maligned animals, such as snakes.

S n a k y   S o l u t i o n s

Snakes are interesting animals. Like all wild animals, they have roles to play in nature. They may look scary. If left alone, however, they seldom harm people.
•Work the math problems to find the numbers that are missing from the sentences.
•Write the correct number in each blank.

1. More than **(5 x 40) x 12** _____ different kinds of snakes live in the world today.

2. The first snakes probably lived about **(5 x 5) x 4** _____ million years ago.

3. The rosy boa, from the American Southwest, has up to **(7 x 8) - 11** _____ rows of scales.

4. Some snakes have as many as **(5 x 10) x 8** _____ pairs of ribs.

5. The anaconda, the largest snake, can grow to **(9 x 13) - 84** _____ feet long.

6. An Indian python many live as long as **(2 x 2) x 5** _____ years.

7. Many snakes like a temperature of about **(20 / 4) x 16** _____ degrees Fahrenheit.

8. Many snakes lay eggs—usually from six to **(7 x 7) - 19** _____ at a time.

9. The spitting cobra of Africa can spit venom a distance of up to **(8 x 8) + 32** _____ inches.

10. The fastest-moving snake, a black mamba from Africa, was timed at **(6 x 12) - 65** ____ miles per hour.

Some people are afraid of snakes.

When people take the time to learn about snakes,
however, often they lose their fear and gain respect.

•**Design a poster asking people to leave snakes alone in their home in the wild.**

Teacher: This worksheet reinforces math skills while focusing on these misunderstood animals.

Text reprinted with permission from the National Association for Humane and Environmental Education, publishers of *KIND News*, P.O. Box 362, East Haddam, CT 06423-0362.

Reprinted with permission from the National Association for Humane and Environmental Education, publishers of KIND News, P.O. Box 362, East Haddam, CT 06423-0362

How Snakes Stay Safe

Snakes have a tough life! They are eaten by many other wild animals.
Many are also killed by people.
So snakes hide–behind rocks, under logs, and down in holes.
Most snakes are also "hidden" by their color.

•Color this snake. Then cut out your snake along the dotted lines and hide
him or her someplace outdoors. Ask a friend to try to find your snake.

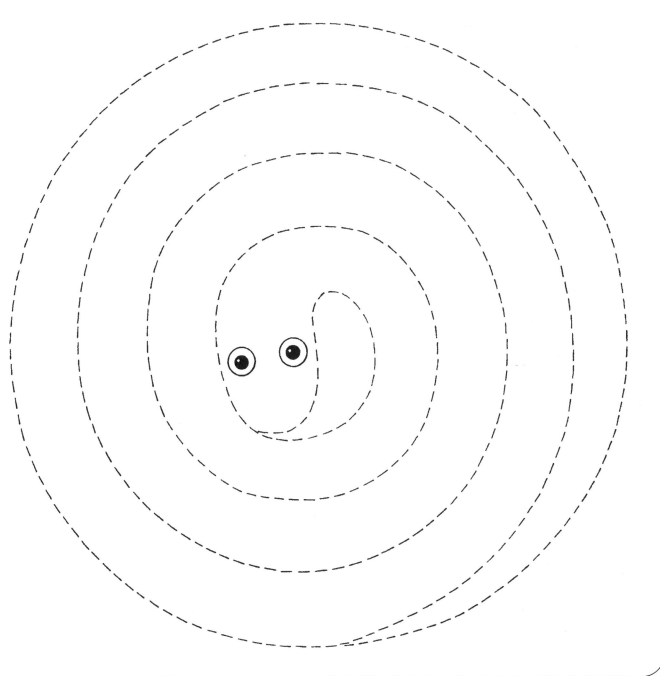

Name..

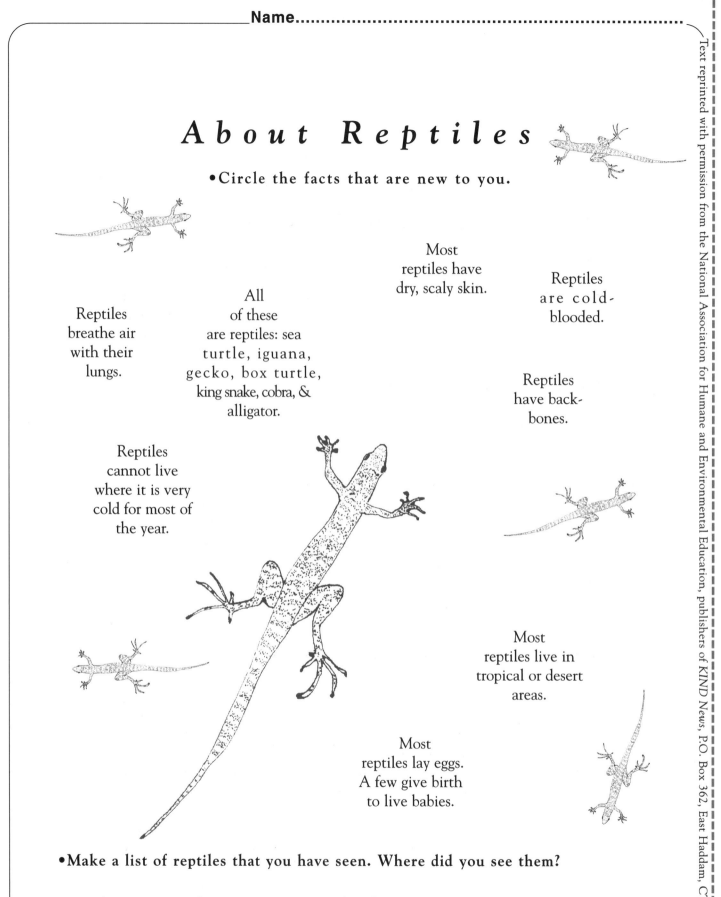

About Reptiles

•Circle the facts that are new to you.

Most reptiles have dry, scaly skin.

Reptiles are cold-blooded.

Reptiles breathe air with their lungs.

All of these are reptiles: sea turtle, iguana, gecko, box turtle, king snake, cobra, & alligator.

Reptiles have back-bones.

Reptiles cannot live where it is very cold for most of the year.

Most reptiles live in tropical or desert areas.

Most reptiles lay eggs. A few give birth to live babies.

•Make a list of reptiles that you have seen. Where did you see them?

Teacher: Use this page to teach about animal groups.

Text reprinted with permission from the National Association for Humane and Environmental Education, publishers of *KIND News*, P.O. Box 362, East Haddam, CT 06423-0362.

40

How's Your
Search Image?

Objective: Children will understand the term "search image."

Concept: Scientists hypothesize that predators form a "search image" of a certain prey species when that species becomes very abundant. Then the predator gets better and better at finding that prey species, because it knows so well what to look for.

You Will Need:
- *Construction paper*
- *Scissors*
- *If you are doing this exercise outdoors, choose a dry, windless day*

What to Do: Think of a prey species that is common in your area. Think of a clear, safe area in your school or schoolyard where a construction paper shape of that species will blend in:

- *green* lizard in *green* grass,
- *brown* mouse on *brown* floor,
- *dark gray* mouse on *asphalt*,
- *brown* rabbit in *brown* dry grass.

Folding the paper, cut out many copies of the prey species' shape.
Better yet, have the children make them!

Distribute these construction paper shapes in your area. Try to leave some where obvious, others a little more hidden. Take the children there and tell them they will walk in a group, in a line, across the area. While walking slowly and quietly, they should be predators and look for their prey, picking up the construction paper shape when they see one.

Try this two or three times. You'll have to redistribute the shapes in between tries, of course, to control variables and ensure that each try starts with the same number of prey available.

CHAPTER EIGHT
There Are Hungry Babies to Feed!

Predator babies must be fed often—it's not easy to be a predator parent!

• As many as 70 percent of coyote pups die, but those who survive need both Mom and Dad to keep them from starving. As the pups scramble to be "first in line," the parents regurgitate already chewed food for their youngsters.

• Great Horned owlets have very devoted parents. In one nest in which there were two four-day-old babies, researchers found the remains of twenty-five different items of prey, including a muskrat and eleven rats, the entire pantry weighing eighteen pounds!

• Bobcat kittens nurse until they are about two months old and then travel with their mother until they are about a year old. Mother bobcat needs to find lots of food to keep the family going.

• On average, a mother bat rears only one youngster per year. Like humans, she nurses her baby from her breasts, so the mother bat has to eat many insects to make her milk.

43

To the forces of diversity, add predators...
far from destroying their prey species, [they] can protect them from extinction
and therby salvage diversity.   —E. O. Wilson

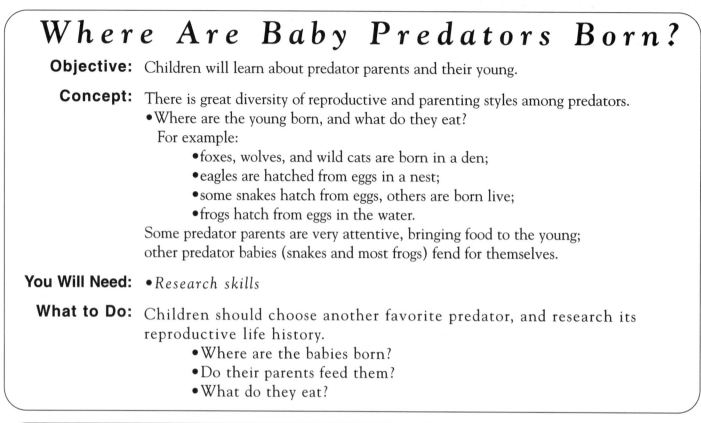

Where Are Baby Predators Born?

Objective: Children will learn about predator parents and their young.

Concept: There is great diversity of reproductive and parenting styles among predators.
  •Where are the young born, and what do they eat?
   For example:
       •foxes, wolves, and wild cats are born in a den;
       •eagles are hatched from eggs in a nest;
       •some snakes hatch from eggs, others are born live;
       •frogs hatch from eggs in the water.
  Some predator parents are very attentive, bringing food to the young;
  other predator babies (snakes and most frogs) fend for themselves.

You Will Need: •*Research skills*

What to Do: Children should choose another favorite predator, and research its reproductive life history.
       •Where are the babies born?
       •Do their parents feed them?
       •What do they eat?

Map a Predator's Home Range

Objective: To make an imaginative map of a predator's home range, and to understand that predators need a lot of space compared to their abundant prey.

Concept: To understand predators, the young scientists in your class need to develop research skills, math skills and mapping skills! This exercise will give them some practice in these areas, plus some fun opportunities to use imagination and art.

You Will Need: •*Large paper*
  •*Writing implements with which to create a map*
  •*Calculator for math*

What to Do: Children will choose their favorite predator and find out the size of its typical home range in your area. Its home range is the area an individual animal will roam over. If that information is hard to come by using school information sources, the staff in your local state wildlife office could help.

Children should also research their predator's natural history and special reproductive requirements. Does it need a rocky hillside for its babies' den? A dense thicket in which to bear young? Large trees in which to build a nest? A cliff to build a nest on?

Children will then draw an imaginary map of their predator's home range, including scale and appropriate habitat features.

CHAPTER NINE
What Happens When Predator Becomes Prey

Rivalry between species can instantly turn a hunter into the hunted. Since the return of the gray wolf to Yellowstone National Park, Glacier National Park, and other parts of northwestern Montana, North America's three premier predators (wolves, grizzlies, and cougars) have been put in the same habitat in the forty-eight states for the first time in decades. According to Howard Quigley of the Hornocker Wildlife Institute in Moscow, Idaho, this provides a great opportunity for predator study. "The wolves and cougars behave just like cats and dogs," he says. "The wolves follow the cougars around, steal their food, and even kill some of the cats."*

On the other hand, wolves and grizzlies interact differently. A lone wolf is no match for a grizzly, but a pack of wolves is a different story—so deaths have occurred on both sides. Sometimes grizzlies chase wolves off kills, other times wolves do the chasing.

In a contest over a carcass, a red fox is no match for a golden eagle. Besides battling foxes for prey, eagles will also grab fox kits from their dens.

Disposition also plays a role in rivalry. For example, at about fifty pounds the wolverine is far from large, but its ferocious nature means it can overcome any carnivore smaller than a grizzly. Biologists also believe the bobcat's aggressive nature allows it to win out over the less aggressive lynx.

*As reported in National Wildlife Magazine, June/July 1998, "When Carnivores Clash," by Gary Turbak.

So how do meat-eaters ever get enough food with so much competition? Surprisingly, they work out some form of sharing. Scientists call this "resource partitioning." It means dividing up habitat, prey, or time so that everyone can get lunch.

Here's how it works in time sharing: red-tailed hawks generally cruise the daytime skies looking for rodents. When night comes they literally turn over the patrolling to the great horned owls.

Here's how it works in habitat sharing: canines prefer open country where they can use their speed and stamina to good advantage; felines, on the other hand, favor wooded, brushy areas ideal for hunting prey by stealth and ambush.

And there are instances where predators actually cooperate in hunting. Biologist Steve Minta of the University of California has seen coyotes and badgers pursuing ground squirrels together. The badger digs into the burrow while the coyote waits at the rear entrance. If a squirrel runs out, the coyote gets it and doesn't share. If the badger reaches the prey first, the coyote goes hungry. Both animals seem to benefit from the relationship: the badger gets a meal when a coyote keeps the squirrels underground, and the coyote gets to eat those that bolt from the burrow.

Biologists are learning more and more about predators, which can only result in a greater appreciation of these important contributors to biodiversity.

Compare Two Predators

Objective: You did this already with predator mammals and predators with wings. Here's a new angle. Have children choose two similar predators. With careful research, they can always find a way that these two species are different and avoid competing.

Concept: To compare in a systematic way; to learn how predator roles differ. Different predator species have different sizes, ranges, habitats, and behavior. These differences mean that predator species, even though they may seem similar, will not usually be in competition with each other.

You Will Need: •*Research and writing skills*

What to Do: Children will make a table for two similar species they wish to compare. They can then circle the differences in range, size, habitat, or behavior that keep the two species from competing. Here are several examples:

Predator:	**badger**	**coyote**
Size:	13-25 lbs.	20-50 lbs.
Range:	Midwest & West	most of U.S.
Habitat:	grasslands, desert	grasslands, desert, forest, suburbs
Method of killing prey:	biting	biting
Usual prey species:	rodents	rodents, rabbits
Other relevant behavior:	(digging into rodent burrows)	(catching prey *above ground*)

Predator:	**bobcat**	**lynx**
Size:	15-35 lbs.	15-30 lbs.
Range:	most of (lower 48 States)	most of (Canada)
Habitat:	forest & desert	forest
Method of killing prey:	biting	biting
Usual prey species:	(small mammals, birds)	(snowshoe hare)
Other relevant behavior:	–	–

Predator:	**cougar**	**wolf**
Size:	80-200 lbs.	70-120 lbs.
Range:	(Western U.S.)	(Canada, Alaska)
Habitat:	(mountains, forest)	(forest, tundra, open areas)
Method of killing prey:	(hide, pounce, bite)	(chase, hunt in packs)
Usual prey species:	deer	deer, caribou, moose
Other relevant behavior:	–	–

CHAPTER TEN
Who's in Control Here, Predator or Prey?

In years when there are higher numbers of meadow voles, foxes will often increase their number of offspring.

Most people assume that predators keep the numbers of prey in control. *But scientists say the prey often controls the predator!* **How can that possibly be? Here's how:**

Most baby predators never grow up—their parents can't find enough food. If they do survive long enough to become independent, often they don't learn fast enough to be efficient predators, and they starve at a young age. Only the most capable young of the most capable parents grow up to become parents themselves. That is called "survival of the fittest."

When prey species become superabundant, as mice and rabbits do at stages of their population cycles, then predators have it a little easier. Fox mothers, for example, may have a bigger litter in a year when mice are superabundant. Also, a larger percentage of their litter might survive, because food is easier for the parents to find.

So that's how the prey are often in control. When they increase their numbers, the predators are then able to do likewise.

Foxy Math

Most people assume that predators keep the numbers of prey in control.
But scientists say the prey often controls the predator! How can that possibly be?

Here's how: •Most baby predators never grow up—their parents can't find enough food.

•If they do survive long enough to become independent, often they don't learn fast enough to be efficient predators, and they starve at a young age.

•Only the *most capable young of the most capable parents* grow up to become parents themselves. That is called "survival of the fittest."

"Fox Valley"

Tell the children to imagine a *beautiful valley with green meadows, farms, and woods.** This valley has about **600 acres**—enough territory for **three fox families** at **200 acres each.**

This year, many mice live in the fields of Fox Valley.
Mother and father fox can catch enough mice so 3 of their babies survive.
How many foxes?
(2 parents + 3 young) x 3 families = **15 foxes**

Next year, many, many mice live in the fields of Fox Valley.
Mother and father fox can catch enough mice so four of their babies survive.
How many foxes?
(2 parents + 4 young) x 3 families = **18 foxes**

Next year, many, many, MANY mice live in the fields of Fox Valley.
Mother and father fox can catch enough mice so five of their babies survive.
How many foxes?
(2 parents + 5 young) x 3 families = **21 foxes**

So the number of mice can "control" the number of foxes!

• Older children can enjoy speculating about *complications*. For example,

1) Some young foxes will undoubtedly leave Fox Valley to find their own territories.

2) After several years of population increase, the mice may get so *crowded* that disease may spread among them

3) OR, the fields with their abundant mice may draw the attention of *hawks and owls.*

Then what will happen to the foxes? There are no quick and easy answers to these questions, but children may enjoy hypothesizing.

Or if it's more relevant to your part of the country, let them imagine a valley with beautiful deserts and rock out-crops.

Teacher: This simplified exercise works well to show youngsters the surprising idea that prey populations can be said to control predator populations.

CHAPTER ELEVEN
Living with Wild Neighbors

Remember when the girl in *Everybody's Somebody's Lunch* checked to be sure the gate to the chicken coop was locked so foxes and raccoons couldn't make a raid? That's what you expect on a farm in the country. But with eight of every ten Americans living in cities or towns that have spread out into wildlife habitat, many animals that used to avoid humans are now coming up to the back door! What do you do about foxes and raccoons, for example, in the backyard?

It helps to have tolerance and understanding of living things. Sometimes red foxes can be so bold they charm us. A hiker along a wooded trail may encounter a fox that doesn't run away but just sits and watches the person. Someone hanging out the laundry may watch as a fox casually ambles through the yard as though it didn't even see the human. Raccoons may seem even tamer. Both foxes and raccoons will raid compost bins and garbage cans. So you can discourage these wild neighbors by not putting meat in compost piles and by tying down the lid to the garbage can. Making a loud noise will usually get a fox to move on. Raccoons may need stronger persuasion like electric fencing to keep them out of the vegetable garden. In keeping them out of chimneys, be very careful not to separate a mother from her babies.

It's best to just watch the wild animals that come close to your house. Putting out food and thus trying to make them pets does more harm than good. Feeding creates overpopulation problems, which in turn can cause disease. For example, distemper and rabies spread rapidly when wild animals live at a high population density. It's better to let wild animals find their own food.

Talk about the wildlife your students have seen near their homes. What did they learn from watching them? What can happen if you make wild animals dependent on you for food? Do your students know whom to call if they see an injured wild animal? Do they know not to move it or touch it? This is important safety information for your students.

Invite someone from your local humane society or a wildlife rehabilitator to talk with your class about living with wild neighbors.

Also an excellent resource is *Wild Neighbors, The Humane Approach to Living with Wildlife* by the Humane Society of the U.S., published by Fulcrum Publishing, Golden, Colorado.

49

Who Are Your Wild Neighbors?

Objective: Children will learn to be observant of everyday, common, local wild animals.

Concept: Children often confuse the term "animals" with "mammals." This will be a good chance to help them realize that insects, worms, reptiles, and birds are also animals. This will also be a good chance to teach them that predators are not always big, fierce mammals.

You Will Need: • *Writing implements*

What to Do: Ask students which wild animals they have seen in their own neighborhood. Even the most urban neighborhoods are likely to have ants, spiders, sparrows, or squirrels.

Make a list of what they have observed. Which are predators? If they have seen ants carrying a dead insect, then the ants were being either *scavengers* (if the insect was already dead) or *predators* (if the ants killed it). All spiders are predators (See Chapter 7). Sparrows eat mostly seeds, but often they catch insects, too. When they catch insects, they are being predators. Squirrels eat mostly nuts, but in the spring they often eat birds' eggs and babies; then, squirrels are being predators.

Make a Telephone List

Objective: Children will gather information about wildlife-related resources in their community. They will present the information in a way that is readily used in a wildlife emergency.

Concept: Most communities have people to call on when there is a problem related to wildlife. For example, wildlife rehabilitators have a license, and training, to catch and help injured animals. Local nature centers, Audubon Societies, or humane societies often have helpful advice. U.S. Fish and Wildlife Service employees are knowledgeable and can sometimes give guidance, as can state game wardens and conservation employees.

You Will Need: • *Writing and art materials*

What to Do: Discuss with children what to do if they see a sick or hurt wild animal. This is a good opportunity to educate them about safety issues. They should never approach a wild animal that is sick or hurt. Such an animal could bite or hurt them. But they can do something constructive and proactive: they can make a list of telephone numbers to call if such a problem came up in their neighborhood. Looking up such agencies and organizations in the phone book is not easy; better to do it in advance of a problem! It is also good practice to check out such numbers ahead of time. Ask what the role of the agency is, and is there a better number to call for wildlife problems. Children will learn about community resources.

The final product might be a short list! Children can decorate it with a picture of a telephone at the top, and their favorite local wild animal at the bottom, and post it by their home phone. They'll feel ready, and empowered.

CHAPTER TWELVE
Protection of Predators

The Migratory Bird Act was a triumph of international cooperation for bird protection.

The Migratory Bird Treaty

This passed in 1918 and its purpose was to put migratory birds, including birds of prey, under federal protection. Before the act was passed, birds were shot all year long, even during the nesting season. When parents are killed, their young die, too. Bird populations could not sustain such terrible overhunting, and several species became extinct in this country.

This year and every year, millions of birds, including hawks, songbirds, sandpipers, swallows, and more fly from Canada through the U.S. and into Mexico for the winter. All three countries now have treaties that protect migratory birds from overhunting.

The Endangered Species Act

The Endangered Species Act is a federal law passed by Congress in 1973. Its purpose is to preserve plant and animal species that are in danger of extinction (endangered species) or that may become so in the near future (threatened species).

Endangered animal species may not be killed, hunted, collected, injured, or otherwise "taken." The law also says that the critical habitat of such species cannot be destroyed. (Why is it that so many predators are on the endangered species list? How many can you think of?)

Endangered snakes, turtles, fish and invertebrates like crayfish, mollusks, and insects need protection, too. They are usually less well-known than the larger mammals and birds. Does your state have endangered reptile, amphibian, or invertebrate species? Unfortunately, many people think they are unimportant and unworthy of protection.

Still, each one plays a role in its environment. Each one is part of our biological heritage, and is part of a living community.

When reptiles, amphibians, and invertebrates become endangered, often it is due to pollution or development of their habitat. Usually protection of these species is brought about by protecting enough of their habitat so that the species can continue to survive.

There are close to 1,000 plant and animal species in the United States alone that are considered endangered or threatened. Why should we care if a species becomes extinct? Because every micro-organism, plant, animal, and human being connects to what scientists call biological diversity or "biodiversity." Every species is a building block in the pyramid of life. There are millions of species on earth, and every single one is important. Even the tiniest single-celled organism is a storehouse of potentially valuable genetic information. Biodiversity provides direct benefits to people. For example, nature is a vital source for new medicines.

Extinction has always been a part of nature. But what concerns scientists now is how *quickly* extinctions are happening. *One species every hour!* That's one guess. But we must be hopeful. One of the great successes of the Endangered Species program is the recovery of our national symbol, the bald eagle. No longer listed as endangered, it is returning to much of its former range.

Make a list of all the things you can do to save endangered species. For example:

• Join a conservation organization that is helping to protect wildlife and wild places.

• Call or write your state wildlife agency and see how you can help endangered species in your state.

• Don't use products that pollute the environment.

• We're sure you can think of many more!

Predators Need Homes, Too!

The most serious problem driving species to extinction is the loss of habitat. An animal's home range size is the area which meets all of its needs for food, water, shelter, and raising its young. Less than 5 percent of the Earth's land surface is protected in national parks. Every day, more and more natural areas are lost to roads, houses, shopping malls, and other human development. We have already lost over half of this country's wetlands, home to nearly half of our federally listed threatened and endangered species. Each time people clear a forest, fill in a wetland, or pave over meadows to build a shopping mall, they are destroying the habitat of untold numbers of plants and animals.

The following will give you an idea of how much habitat different predators need. (The amount varies with location and whether it is a male or female. *These are estimates.*)

Average Habitat Requirements for Selected Predators

- **Grizzly Bear**—as much as 800 square miles
- **Gray Wolf**—10 square miles for *one* wolf (minimum in Great Lakes)
- **Gray Wolf**—460 square miles (average *pack* territory in Montana)
- **Fisher**—from 1 to 15 square miles (depending on location)
- **Mountain Lion**—from 30 to 300 square miles (for solitary animal)
- **Red fox**—25 acres
- **Skunk**—40 acres

Sources: *The Fragmented Forest* by L. D. Harris (University of Chicago Press, 1984) and The Predator Project.

Forest carnivores such as the lynx, wolverine, fisher, and marten are not getting the attention they deserve. They desperately need protection from trapping. They need large, roadless forests with mature trees, but these regions are fast disappearing.

There are places in the U.S. where wildlife is protected in areas designated as Wilderness and in our National Parks. But you might be surprised to learn that while National Wildlife Refuges were originally established as "inviolate sanctuaries," those words have become meaningless. Many refuges are used for target practice by the military, oil and gas operations go on in others, and even hunting and trapping are allowed in more and more refuges. Some improvements have been made, but not enough.

The world's first refuge for the protection of birds of prey was established in 1934 in Pennsylvania.

The Hawk Mountain Sanctuary, which is privately funded, has grown to 2,200 acres located north of Reading. It is situated on the very ridge where migrating hawks and other raptors were once shot out of the sky by the thousand. Now avid bird watchers can observe over 24,000 migrants each fall, and today close to 70 different species nest in the Sanctuary.

In 1993 the Snake River Birds of Prey National Conservation Area was established just southwest of Boise, Idaho, by the U.S. Department of the Interior and the Bureau of Land Management. Its 485,000 acres run along 80 miles of the Snake River, with its steep, craggy cliffs and abundance of ground squirrels and jack rabbits. Reportedly, it has the densest population of nesting raptors in North America, if not the world. More than 800 pairs of falcons, eagles, hawks, and owls gather there each spring to mate and raise their young. These are just two of such refuges.

Bats have their defenders, too. Dr. Merlin D. Tuttle founded Bat Conservation International many years ago. He and his associates protect caves where bats roost, putting up metal grates that keep people out while letting bats move in and out freely.

It is estimated that one-third of all endangered species are found on privately owned land. That is why organizations such as the Nature Conservancy, the National Audubon Society, and the Humane Society of the U.S. Wildlife Land Trust, to name just a few, buy or accept as donations gifts of land that are significant habitats.

The Return of Predators

It is costly, but in some places where native predators have been exterminated there are efforts to bring them back. (How much better not to let them disappear in the first place!)

For example, restoring timber wolves to Yellowstone National Park and Idaho was a long-time dream of conservationists. And in the winter of 1994-95 their dream came true. The U.S. Fish and Wildlife Service began its first translocation of Canadian wolves to former wolf habitat in Wyoming and Idaho. Forty-one wolves were transplanted to the Park. Although one was shot almost immediately, the rest have more than doubled their numbers and have formed more than a half-dozen well-established packs. But the fear and misunderstanding of local ranchers still exist. There are formidable legal battles to fight before the reintroduction project can be called a success. These could affect similar plans for Olympic National Park.

In 1984 the Peregrine Fund was established in Boise, Idaho. Now it has become the World Center for Birds of Prey. Two hundred different species of raptors reproduce at the Center, and their young are released into the wild in the U.S. and internationally. For example, the Center has released over 4,000 peregrine falcons in twenty-eight states.

Other projects in other parts of the country involve returning the red wolf to North Carolina, the Mexican gray wolf to Arizona, black-footed ferrets to Wyoming, and California condors to California.

Getting your class involved in these projects makes education really fun. If you would like more information on reintroductions, you'll find the address for the Office of the U.S. Fish and Wildlife Service nearest you in the Directory of Regional Offices in the back of this book.

Map YOUR Home Range!

Objective: Children will learn the concept of home range— an important concept in wildlife biology—while practicing mapping skills.

Concept: All animals have a "home range"—the area they travel over regularly to find food, water, shelter, and raise a family. Students will have learned from Activity 2, Chapter 8, that predators typically have a much larger home range than their prey species. That's because a herbivore's food is much more abundant than that of a predator.
Students will have a "home range," too—the areas they usually visit for visiting friends and relatives, buying food, going to school, library, sports, and other activities.

You Will Need: •A simplified map of your local area

What to Do: Have students use a local map to label places that are important to them— friends' homes, fast food restaurants, school, library, sports facilities, and other activities.

Then, they should draw a prominent line around their home ranges. They can try to calculate how much area their home range is, and compare it to the list of predator home ranges.

53

Use the World Wide Web to Be an Activist

Objective: Children will learn how to become activists, writing a letter expressing their opinions in support of predator protection.

Concept: "Activists" tell other people their opinions, explaining why they care about animals, and urging others to join the fight to save animals. Activists are politically active, trying to influence policy. Several wildlife protection organizations mobilize citizen support for current legislation, urging activists to write to politicians. They give activists the facts necessary to write an effective letter.

You Will Need:
- *Writing materials*
- *Access to the World Wide Web*

What to Do: Visit the Website of the **National Wildlife Federation** at http://www.nwf.org or **The Predator Project** at http://www.wildrockies.org/predproj/

These will tell you about pending wildlife- or predator-related legislation. They will also give facts and formats for an effective letter, and even the name and address of your senator or representative. Politicians will nearly always respond directly and relevantly to citizen letters about legislation.

Where Do Birds Go in Migration?

Objective: Children will learn that bird migration transcends political boundaries, so their protection requires international cooperation. Birds don't stop at the border! That's why the Migratory Bird Act was a triumph of international cooperation for bird protection.

Concept: Many birds make long international trips each year. Some go from Canada, through the United States and Mexico, all the way through Central America to South America, and back. Many bird books have maps showing migratory routes and flyways. The lines on these routes represent "rivers of birds" in the sky! Many small songbirds migrate at night, using the stars, and possibly the earth's magnetic fields, to find their way.

You Will Need:
- *Paper for a large wall-sized mural*
- *Yarn of different colors*

What to Do: Children will enjoy making a mural-size map of North and South America. They should *choose a songbird*, research its migration, and tape colored yarn marking its migratory route on the map.

Despite the protection of the Migratory Bird Act, many migratory birds are *declining* in number due to habitat destruction in both North and South America. Perhaps a representative of a local Audubon Society or bird club could talk to your class about this issue.

What Is "Endangered"?
What Is "Extinct"?

Objective: To find out what students know about these terms; to enhance and enrich their understanding.

Concept: If a species is endangered, its population is dangerously low and it is in danger of becoming extinct. If a species is extinct, it exists no more; the last member of the species has died.

You Will Need: •*Writing materials*

What to Do: Ask students what these terms mean. Are their answers at all close to the definitions given here? Do they know which species are endangered in their state? There are **state endangered species** and **federally endangered species**. An animal could be very rare in your state, but be more common elsewhere in the U. S. In that case, it could be a state endangered species, but not a federally endangered species. Have any students in the class ever seen an endangered species in the wild? In a zoo?

•Children could make a list of the endangered species and extinct species they could think of; then add to the list with further research.

Revisit "Paper Chain"
and "Ecology Blocks"
from Chapter 3

Objective: Have children use the ecology symbols (the "Paper Chain" and "Ecology Blocks") they made back in Chapter 3 to demonstrate dramatically why we don't want endangered species to become extinct.

Concept: Children can show how a chain is shortened if a link is lost. If the predator in their "food chain" becomes extinct, the chain of life is diminished. Links in the paper chain can be ripped, letting the species they represent flutter to the floor. Children should only do this to their art work if they want to!

You Will Need: •*Paper chain and ecology blocks from Chapter 3*

What to Do: With their ecology blocks, children can demonstrate how a pyramid is diminished when the top predator is lost. Prey species may multiply. Then, prey species may overeat the plant at the base of the food pyramid. Each block or link *represents a species in the chain of life*, or the pyramid of life.

When a species becomes extinct, the chain or pyramid is diminished.

CHAPTER THIRTEEN
Are WE Predators?

Humans are the most powerful predators in the world because we have the power to kill any wild animal we wish, even to wipe out an entire species.

People who choose not to eat meat are vegetarians (herbivores). People who do eat meat and veggies (omnivores) usually buy the meat at the store. So a coyote eating a deer is no different from a person eating a steak. Neither is "bad" or "mean."

Class Discussion of Hunting, Vegetarians, etc.

Why are some people vegetarians?

Ask your students how they feel about *hunting*.

Talk about *native people* hunting.

What is the difference between *hunting for food* and hunting for *sport trophies*?

Is it right to try to *eliminate* a species?

• Encourage many different opinions. There should be no "winning" side.

• Students should be challenged to think more deeply about their arguments.

Teacher: This subject makes for lively class discussion!

Supermarket Scramble

Objective: Students will learn about the origins of our food. Are we *carnivores* or *herbivores*?

Concept: Many people are omnivores, eating both meat and vegetable matter. Vegetarians are herbivores. Does your class have some of each?

You Will Need: • *Small-size items from the supermarket that can be handled without damage, like cans of tuna, salmon, and ham; a box of spaghetti; a box of sugar; bags of rice and flour; cans of vegetables; a jar of peanut butter.*

What to Do: Have the students tell you where the food comes from. Which ocean do tuna and salmon come from? Are they predators? Many children will not know that spaghetti is made from wheat, or how and where rice or vegetables are grown, or what sugar is made of. What is their favorite food, what is it made of, and where is it grown? Our food is similar to that of wild animals, in that it all comes from other living things, plants or animals. People just preprocess their food more than animals do. Do your students feel like predators when they eat a hamburger?

Children can sort the food items into two categories, *plant* and *animal*, once they know the source of each.

CHAPTER FOURTEEN
Death in Nature and Loss of a Pet

Perhaps one reason people have feared and persecuted predators is that predation is violent and ends in death. Civilized people abhor violence and most people dread death, their own and that of their loved ones. In Western society, death is considered a tragedy and a waste.

But in nature, death is an every-hour, everyday occurrence, and *nothing* is wasted. Most baby animals never get to live out their life span, dying young of predation or starvation. Even if not eaten, they are recycled into soil by worms, insects, and bacteria. Then plants grow from the soil and are eaten by herbivores, which in turn are eaten by carnivores. An individual wild animal's life is one small, temporary part of the great web of life, which continuously reweaves itself with different individuals.

> THERE IS SOMETHING INFINITELY HEALING IN THE REPEATED REFRAINS OF NATURE—
>
> THE ASSURANCE THAT DAWN COMES AFTER THE NIGHT AND SPRING COMES AFTER WINTER.
>
> *–Rachel Carson*

In the story Granny tells in *Everybody's Somebody's Lunch*, we read that "the death of the hare is the gift of life for the hawk." There is a constant rebirth in nature as living creatures survive on those that have died; it is an endless circle of life.

Many times, however, it is difficult for us to accept the death of a cherished animal. When our dog or cat dies we are heartbroken because we have lost a beloved friend. Because the loss of a pet may be a child's first experience with death, experts advise being open and honest with children. Here are some helpful things to say:

• All living creatures in this world are born and finally die. It is perfectly natural.

• It is okay for you to cry and feel really bad for a while about the loss of a pet.

• You are not alone. Your veterinarian or local humane society may know of a nearby support group.

• Say good-bye while your pet is still alive; grieving afterwards is all right, too.

• Maybe a little memorial service will help you realize that your pet is gone.

• You can put a wood or stone marker or some flowers on its grave if you choose to bury your pet.

• You can write a poem or compose a song in your pet's memory.

• After a while, think about getting a new pet, but don't do it until you're ready to give your love to a new pet, not to try to replace the one that's gone.

• And don't think it's disloyal to try and find a new friend. You will never forget the pet that died, but there are many abandoned and homeless dogs and cats in shelters who need your love and a good home.

Discuss the Death of a Pet

Objective: For children to discuss the loss of the girl's cat, in the story *Everybody's Somebody's Lunch*. This could lead into a discussion of the death of their pets, too.

Concept: The death of anything you care about is a painful loss, but the pain diminishes with time, caring, and sharing.

You Will Need: *• Empathy and understanding*

What to Do: Ask children if they have ever felt sad because a pet died. When they tell their stories, here are some helpful things to say: It's OK to feel sad about it. You loved your pet a lot, didn't you? What good times with your pet can you remember? Why is a pet such a good friend?

Discuss a Dead Wild Animal

Objective: To have children discuss whether they have ever seen a dead wild animal.

Concept: Death is part of life, and part of nature, and part of predation, but seldom discussed. Perhaps an occasional discussion about its occurrence, and a child's reaction to it, could help normalize the concept of death, especially when the death occurs to a wild animal with which the child was not emotionally involved.

You Will Need: *• Empathy, caring, and interest*

What to Do: Ask children if they have ever seen a dead wild animal. What did they observe about it? What kind of animal was it? What killed it? How did they feel about it? What happened to the animal later?

You might conclude with this idea: animals that are not eaten by a predator or scavenger turn slowly into soil after they die.
Insects, fungi, and bacteria help turn a dead animal into soil. This takes time, and is not always a pleasant thing to see or smell.

But eventually, new plants will grow from the soil,
      and herbivores will eat the plants,
            and predators will eat the herbivores in an endless,
                  natural cycle of life, death, and new life again.

The Outdoor Classroom

IMPARTIAL SYMPATHY TOWARD ALL CREATURES,
REGARDLESS OF THEIR DIET,
IS AN ATTITUDE OF THE CULTIVATED MIND.
—*Durward L. Allen, Wolf Biologist*

As great as the indoor classroom is for learning, the great outdoors offers learning, too. Only by first-hand knowledge, observation, and experience will children come to understand the cycles of life and death of which predation is part.

Observation of nature near a school presents a challenge in some circumstances. Many urban schools are surrounded by asphalt. But sometimes plants and trees push their way up through the asphalt, and where there are plants there often will be the start of a food chain.

You and your students can look for holes chewed in the leaves, a sign of herbivores at work! Often they will be small caterpillars or other insects. Where there are many insects, often a spider waits, the predator in the food web. Where there are cracks in the sidewalk, there may be ants. Something as small as an ant offers a world of learning.

Sometimes there are parks or vacant lots near schools. These can be productive places in which to have students carry our their nature studies, as long as they are safe. A check should be made for safety hazards first, with educational opportunities next in your priorities.

More and more nature centers are being developed around the edges of urban areas. Perhaps there is one near you. They offer excellent educational programs.

If there is a park near your school, and it has trees, often it also has squirrels. Children will love to observe them.

Nature observation, combined with the theme of predation, makes a powerful combination to motivate children to read, write, do math, acquire science skills, and work with their peers on a fact-finding team. Because of its powerful emotional content, there is also a good chance that this combination will guide your students down a lifelong road of science literacy and independent, self-motivated learning.

A Predator Glossary

adaptable able to change to fit the situation.

amphibian a member of a class of vertebrate animals that includes frogs and salamanders. Most members of this class have thin, moist skin and live in moist places. Many start out as a jelly-like egg in the water, become a tadpole, and end up on land breathing air.

arthropod a group of animals with jointed legs and a protective body covering. Examples are insects, crabs, lobsters, and spiders.

biodiversity the variety and variability of living things.

burrow a hole or tunnel dug by an animal to make a home to live in.

cache a hiding place for food.

canid a family of carnivorous dogs.

carnivore an animal whose diet is mostly meat.

carrion the meat of a dead animal.

diurnal active during the day.

ecosystem all the living things of an area, together with their physical environment.

endangered threatened with extinction.

extinction dying out or ceasing to exist.

feral reverting to a wild state after being domesticated.

food chain a community of plants and animals joined by the flow of food energy from one to another through the consumption of one organism by another.

gene a part of a molecule that determines heredity.

habitat the natural surrounding that provides an animal with its food, water, shelter, and place to bear and raise its young.

herbivore an animal whose diet is mostly plants; usually a prey animal.

home range the area over which an individual animal regularly travels to find food, shelter, and water.

invertebrate an animal without a backbone.

mammal a warm-blooded animal that nurses its young with milk.

marine of or related to the sea.

marsh a wetland normally covered by shallow water all year.

nocturnal active at night.

omnivore an animal that eats both plants and animals.

opportunist an animal that will eat almost anything.

pack a group of animals that live and hunt together.

plumage the feathers of a bird.

pollutant any material that poisons soil, water or air.

predator an animal that hunts other animals for food.

prey an animal that is caught by another animal for food.

rabies a disease caused by a virus that can affect all mammals.

range the area in which an entire species is found (compare with home range; these two concepts are often confused).

refuge a place that provides protection or shelter.

reintroduction returning an organism to a region it once inhabited but from which it has been absent.

scat droppings of feces.

scavenger an animal that eats dead animals it did not kill.

search image an image of an object presumably held in the mind to help find that object.

shorebird a bird that frequents the shores of coastal or inland bodies of water.

species a group into which plants and animals are divided based on shared characteristics and the ability to reproduce their own kind.

talon the sharp, curved claw of a bird of prey.

Bibliography

It would be impossible to list the many books that cover predator/prey relationships as well as histories of individual predator and prey animals. Your local library is undoubtedly richly endowed with many books on these many subjects. The following are just a few suggestions:

Bauer, Erika. 1994. *Wild Dogs: The Wolves, Coyotes and Foxes of North America*. Chronicle Books, San Francisco

Caduto, Michael J. and Joseph Bruchac. 1991. *Keepers of the Animals; Native Stories and Wildlife Activities for Children*. Fifth House Publishers, Saskatoon

Fair, Jeff. 1990. *The Great American Bear*. Northwood Press, Inc., Minocqua, WI

Grady, Wayne. 1994. *The Nature of Coyotes, Voice of the Wilderness*. Greystone Books, Vancouver

Greene, Harry W. 1997. *Snakes*. University of California Press, Berkeley, Los Angeles, London

Grice, Gordon. 1998. *The Red Hourglass, Lives of the Predators*. Delacorte Press, Bantam Doubleday Dell Publishing Group, Inc., New York

Henry, J. David. 1986. *Red Fox*. Smithsonian Institution Press, New York, London

The Humane Society of the United States. 1997. *Wild Neighbors, the Humane Approach to Living with Wildlife*. Fulcrum Publishing, Golden, CO

Landau, Diana and Shelley Stump. 1994. *Living with Wildlife*. Sierra Club Books, San Francisco

Lembke, Janet. 1992. *Dangerous Birds*. Lyons & Burford, Publishers, New York

Lopez, Barry. 1978. *Of Wolves and Men*. Charles Scribner's Sons, New York

McNamee, Thomas. 1984. *The Grizzly Bear*. Alfred A. Knopf, New York

Mowat, Farley. 1983. *Never Cry Wolf*. Seal Books, McLelland and Stewart-Bantam, Toronto

National Geographic Society. 1983. *The Wonder of Birds*. Washington, D. C.

Poole, Alan F. 1989. *Ospreys, a Natural and Unnatural History*. Cambridge University Press, Cambridge

Prince J.H. 1980. *How Animals Hunt*. Elsevier/Nelson Books, New York

Savage, Candace. 1988. *Wolves*. Sierra Club Books, San Francisco

Tuttle, Merlin D. 1988. *America's Neighborhood Bats*. University of Texas Press, Austin

Whitfield, Dr. Philip. 1978. *The Hunters*. Simon and Schuster, New York

More Books about Predators and Prey

Books about Birds of Prey:

Richards, Alan. 1995. *Birds of Prey: Hunters of the Sky.* Courage Press.

Scholz, Floyd. 1993. *Birds of Prey.* Stackpole Books.

Smithsonian Institution. 1990. *Hawks, Eagles, and Falcons of North America.*

Smithsonian Institution. 1988. *North American Owls: Biology and Natural History.*

Snyder, Noel and Helen. 1991. *Raptors: North American Birds of Prey.* Voyager Press.

Toups, Connie. 1990. *Owls.* Voyager Press.

Weisensaul, Scott. 1996. *Raptors: The Birds of Prey.* Lyons & Burford.

Books about Fish:

Paxton, John R. and William Eschermeyer. 1995. *Encyclopedia of Fishes.* Academic Press.

Books about Insects:

Brackenbury, John. 1995. *Insects: Life Cycles and the Seasons.* Blandford.

Evans, Howard Ensign. 1993. *Life on a Little-Known Planet: A Biologist's View of Insects and Their World.* Lyons & Burford.

Books about Reptiles and Amphibians:

Bauchot, Roland. 1997. *Snakes: A Natural History.* Sterling.

Halliday, Kim and Kraig Adler. *Encyclopedia of Reptiles and Amphibians.*

Books about Spiders (for Juveniles and Adults)

Compiled by Daniel T. Jennings, Principal Research Entomologist, USDA, Forest Service (Ret.), P.O. Box 130, Garland, Maine 04939-0130; and Cynthia A. Jennings, Librarian, Orono Public Library, Orono, Maine 04473; (Revised 9 September 1997).

Bailey, Donna. 1992. *Animal World. Spiders.* Austin, TX: Steck-Vaughn Co. 33 pp.

Bailey, Jill. 1989. *The Life Cycle of A Spider.* NY: The Bookwright Press. 32 pp.

Barrett, Norman. 1989. *Picture Library. Spiders.* NY: Franklin Watts, Inc. 32 pp.

Biel, Timothy Levi. 1991. *Spiders.* Zoobook Series, Mankato, MN: Creative Education, Inc. 24 pp.

Browning, John G. 1989. *Tarantulas.* Neptune City, NJ: T. F. H. Publications, Inc. 96 pp.

Chinery, Michael. 1991. *Spider.* Troll Associates. 32 pp.

Cole, Joanna. 1995. *Spider's Lunch: All About Garden Spiders.* NY: All Aboard Reading. Grosset & Dunlap.

David, Al. 1987. *Tarantulas. A Complete Introduction.* Neptune, NJ: T. F. H. Publications, Inc. 96 pp.

Dewey, Jennifer Owings. 1993. *Spiders Near and Far.* NY: Dutton Children's Books. 48 pp.

French, Vivian. 1994. *Spider Watching.* Cambridge, MA: Candlewick Press.

Gibbons, Gail. 1993. *Spiders.* NY: Holiday House. 32 pp.

Hancock, Kathleen and John. 1992. *Tarantulas: Keeping and Breeding Arachnids in Captivity.* Somerset, England: R. & A. Publishing Ltd. 147 pp.

Hawcock, David and Lee Montgomery. 1994. *Spider.* Series Title: *Bouncing Bugs, A Read-About, Fold-Out, and Pop-Up.* NY: Random House, Inc. 18 pp.

Henwood, Chris. 1988. *Keeping Minibeasts: Spiders.* NY: Franklin Watts, Inc. 29 pp.

Hillyard, Paul. 1995. *A Look Inside Spiders and Scorpions.* China: A Joshua Morris Book. Reader's Digest Young Families, Inc., Stewart Crowley & Associates. 19 pp.

Hopf, Alice L. 1990. *Spiders*. NY: Cobblehill Books, E. P. Dutton. 64 pp.

Jennings, Terry. 1989. *Junior Science. Spiders*. NY: Gloucester Press. 24 pp.

Julivert, Maria Angels. 1992. *The Fascinating World of . . . Spiders*. Hauppauge, NY: Barron's Educational Series, Inc. 32 pp.

Kendall, Cindy. 1995. *Spiders*. A Dial Nature Notebook Pop-up. NY: Dial Books for Young Readers. 32 pp.

La Bonte, Gail. 1991. *The Tarantula*. Minneapolis, MN: Dillon Press. 58 pp.

Lane, Margaret and Barbara Firth. 1994. *The Spider*. NY: A Pied Piper Book. Dial Books for Young Readers. 32 pp.

Levi, Herbert W. and Lorna R. 1987. *A Guide to Spiders and Their Kin*. NY: A Golden Nature Guide. Golden Press. 160 pp.

Lovett, Sarah. 1991. *Extremely Weird Spiders*. Santa Fe, NM: John Muir Publications. 48 pp.

Markle, Sandra. 1994. *Outside and Inside Spiders*. NY: Bradbury Press. 40 pp.

Martin, Louise. 1988. *Black Widow Spiders*. Vero Beach, FL: Rourke Enterprises, Inc. 24 pp.

_____. *Fishing Spiders*. Vero Beach, FL: Rourke Enterprises, Inc. 24 pp.

Milne, Lorus J. and Margery. 1992. *Insects and Spiders*. NY: Doubleday. 45 pp.

Morris, Dean. 1991. *Spiders*. Austin, TX: Steck-Vaughn Co. 47 pp.

Murray, Peter. 1992. *Spiders*. Chicago, IL: The Child's World, Inc., Encyclopedia Britannica Educational Corp. 32 pp.

Nielsen, Nancy J. 1990. *The Black Widow Spider*. NY: Crestwood House. 47 pp.

O'Toole, Christopher. 1990. *Insects and Spiders*. NY: The Encyclopedia of the Animal World. Facts on File, Inc. 96 pp.

Parsons, Alexander. 1990. *Amazing Spiders*. NY: Eyewitness Juniors, Alfred A. Knopf. 29 pp.

Petty, Kate. 1990. *Spiders*. NY: Franklin Watts. 30 pp.

Pringle, Lawrence P. 1990. *The Golden Book of Insects and Spiders*. Racine, WI: Golden Book. 45 pp.

Rankin, Wayne and Jerry G. Walls. 1994. *Tarantulas and Scorpions: Their Care in Captivity*. Neptune, NJ: T. F. H. Publications, Inc. 65 pp.

Robinson, Fay. 1996. *Mighty Spiders*. NY: Cartwheel Books. Scholastic, Inc. 32 pp.

Schnieper, Claudia. 1989. *Amazing Spiders*. Minneapolis, MN: Carolrhoda Books. 48 pp.

Simons, Jamie and Scott. 1991. *Why Spiders Spin. A Story of Arachne*. Englewood Cliffs, NJ: Silver Burdett Press, Inc. [Unpaged].

Souza, D.M. 1991. *Eight Legs*. Minneapolis, MN: Carolrhoda Books. 40 pp.

Tesar, Jenny. 1993. *Spiders*. Woodbridge, CT: Blackbirch Press, Inc. 64 pp.

Time-Life Books. 1993. *Insects and Spiders. Understanding Science and Nature*. Time-Life Inc. 152 pp.

Vansant, Rhonda and Barbara L. Dondiego. 1995. *Moths, Butterflies, Other Insects and Spiders: Science in Art, Song, and Play*. Blue Ridge Summit, PA: TAB Books. 100 pp.

Waricha, Jean. 1992. *101 Wacky Facts about Bugs and Spiders*. NY: Scholastic, Inc. 96 pp.

Webb, Ann. 1992. *The Proper Care of Tarantulas*. Neptune City, NJ: T. F. H. Publications, Inc. 288 pp.

Wildlife Education Fund. 1993. *Spiders*. San Diego, CA: Wildlife Education, Ltd. 24 pp.

Wolf, Jill. 1990. *Spiders and Scorpions*. Yellow Springs, OH: Antioch Publishing Co. [Unpaged].

World Wide Web Sites

The following Web sites are relevant to the study of predators and prey, and are suitable for children:

Bears:
http://library.advanced.org/11922/bears/bears.html
This site contains wav.audio files that you can click to hear the roar of several types of bears. All you need to know about this large carnivore: what it eats, how it lives, and how long it lives.

Coyotes:
http://www.ngpc.state.ne.us/wildlife/coyote.html
This site includes information on the coyote's habitat, habits, mortality, foods, and an audio file of its howls.

Foxes:
http://www.floodlight-findings.com/2redfox.html
The red fox's scientific name is Vulpes Vulpes, which means "Fox Fox." They're good at catching mice, very good, because they can hear one squeal from almost 150 yards away.

Garter Snakes:
http://klaatu.oit.umass.edu:80/umext/snake/cgarter.html
http://www.eecs.tufts.edu/~cabotsch/bulloughs/vertebrates/reptiles/garter-snake.html
Interesting information about the garter snake for children.

Raptors:
http://www.kn.pacbell.com/wired/fil/pages/huntbirdsofp.html
Here you will find a fact-filled treasure hunt for birds of prey as well as links to many other sites about raptors.

Shrews:
http://library.advanced.org/11922/mammals/shrews.html
A brief overview of these active, mouselike animals that feed primarily on insects and worms but also eat mice.

Spiders Home Page:
http:www.powerup.com.au/~glen/spiders/a.html
This site contains spider information, interesting spider facts, poems, stories and art. It even has easy recipes for chocolate spiders and cookie spiders and a spider worksheet.

Wolves in the Wild:
http://www.angelfire.com/ma/steveswolves
Characteristics of the gray wolf and links to other wolf pages. Did you know that the wolf's long legs allow it to run at speeds of up to 45 miles per hour?

Bat Conservation International:
http://www.batcon.org

Hawk Mountain Sanctuary:
http://www.hawkmountain.org/directry.html

International Wolf Center:
http://www.wolf.org
National Audubon Society (The Watchlist):
http://www.audubon.org

Partners in Flight (Migratory Songbirds):
http://www.pwrc.nbs.gov/pif

The Peregrine Fund (Peregrine Falcon, an Endangered Species):
http://peregrinefund.org/IntroPF.html

The Predator Project:
http://www.wildrockies.org/predproj

Snake River Birds of Prey National Conservation Area: http://www.id.blm.gov.bopnca

U.S. Fish and Wildlife Service (Endangered Species): http://www.fws.gov

World Wildlife Fund:
http://www.wwf.org

Teaching Resources

The American Museum of Natural History in New York City has many science-oriented activities that foster observation skills in children. For example, *Biodiversity: It Takes All Kinds to Make a World* is a 16-page magazine of word puzzles, picture searches, and games. Visit the Biodiversity Center's website at http://research.amnh.org/biodiversity.

Bat Conservation International has a variety of educational materials, from a set of slides to activity books. Call 1-800-538-BATS; their website is www.batcon.org.

Biological Diversity, a curriculum for teachers and interpreters designed for visiting national parks with pre-visit, on-site and post-visit activities (adaptable by teachers for other places), is available from National Parks and Conservation Association, 1776 Massachussetts Ave. NW, Washington, DC 20036.

British Columbia S.P.C.A. Education Division: **"The Coyote Kit,"** a Teacher's Guide and Student Activities Manual for Intermediate Level. 322-470 Granville Street, Vancouver, B.C. V6C1V5; (604) 681-3379; FAX: (604) 681-7022; e-mail: info@spca.bc.ca

Dog-Eared Publications, Nancy Field, Publisher and Wildlife Biologist, offers a variety of **"Discovery" books for grades 3-6.** P.O. Box 620863, Middletown, WI 53562-0863. Phone and FAX: (608) 831-1410; e-mail: field@midplains.net

Endangered & Threatened Wildlife and Plants: the actual current list of endangered plants and animals as printed by the U.S. Government Printing Office is available from Endangered Species Division, U.S. Fish and Wildlife Service, P.O. Box 45, Federal Building, Fort Snelling, Twin Cities, MN 55111.

Endangered Species: Rare and Wild. Part of Ranger Rick's *Naturescope* series, this book is a collection of activities and background information aimed at grades K-7. For information contact National Wildlife Federation, 1412 16th St. NW, Washington, DC 20036-2266.

Hawk Mt. Sanctuary has a Teacher's Guide to Raptors and the Central Appalachian Forest for grades 6-8. It includes natural history background and student activities. Contact Annette Turner, HMS, 1700 Hawk Mt. Road, Kempton, PA 19529. Website: www.hawkmountain. org

International Wolf Center, "Wolf Watchers" educational program, curriculum, newspapers, etc. 1396 Highway 169, Ely, MN 55371; 1-800-359-9653; Web site: www.wolf.org

National Association for Humane and Environmental Education (NAHEE), publishers of *KIND News,* a monthly classroom newspaper for the elementary grades. To subscribe, or for more information, contact NAHEE, P.O. Box 362, East Haddam, CT 06423-0362; (860) 434-8666; FAX: (860) 434-9579; e-mail: nahee@nahee. org.; Web site: www.nahee.org

Project Wild: K-12 Activity Guides and Workshops to develop awareness, knowledge, skills, and commitment to result-informed decisions, responsible behavior and constructive actions concerning wildlife and the environment. 707 Conservation Lane, Gaithersburg MD 20878; (301) 493-5447.

Curriculum Guides for Teachers

National Association for Humane and Environmental Education: *KIND News, Teacher's Magazine.* P.O. Box 362, East Haddam, CT 06423-0362.

National Audubon Society, *Audubon Adventures Teacher's Resource Manual,* 1997.

National Wildlife Federation. *NatureScope. Incredible Insects; Amazing Mammals; Endangered Species; Reptiles & Amphibians.*

Western Regional Environmental Education Council. *Project Wild. Aquatic Project Wild.*

Conservation Groups

Bat Conservation International
P.O. Box 162603; Austin, TX 78716-2603;
(512) 327-9721

Cornell Laboratory of Ornithology
159 Sapsucker Woods Rd., Ithaca, NY 14850;
800-843-2473

Declining Amphibian Populations Task Force
e-mail: DAPTF@opew.ac.UK

Defenders of Wildlife
1101 14th St. NW, Suite 1400, Washington, D.C.
20005; (202) 682-9400

Hawk Mountain Sanctuary Association
RT. 2, Box 191, Kempton, PA 19529; (610) 756-6961

Hawkwatch International
P.O. Box 660, Salt Lake City, UT 84110;
(801) 524-8520

The Humane Society of the United States
2100 L St. NW, Washington, D.C. 20037;
(202) 452-1100

International Wolf Center
1396 Highway 169, Ely, MN 55732; 1-800-359-9653

Manomet Bird Observatory
P.O. Box 1770, Manomet, MA 22345

Mountain Lion Foundation
P.O. Box 1896; Sacramento, CA 95812;
(916) 442-2666

National Audubon Society
700 Broadway, New York, NY 10003; (212) 979-3126

National Wildlife Federation
1400 16th St. NW, Washington, D.C. 20036; (202)
797-6800

The Nature Conservancy
1815 N. Lynn St., Arlington, VA 22209;
(703) 841-5300

The Peregrine Fund, World Center for Birds of Prey
566 West Flying Hawk Lane, Boise, ID 83709; (208)
362-3716

Point Reyes Bird Observatory
4990 Shoreline Highway, Stinson Beach, CA 94924

Predator Project
P.O. Box 6733, Bozeman, MT 59771; (406) 587-3389

Restore: The North Woods
P.O. Box 440, Concord, MA 01742; (508) 287-0320

Sierra Club
85 Second St., Second Floor, San Francisco, CA
94105; (415) 977-5500

Snake River Birds of Prey National Conservation Area
Bureau of Land Management/Lower Snake River
District/Boise Field Office
3948 Development Ave., Boise, ID 83705;
(208) 383-3300

Wild Canines Unlimited
Antioch New England Graduate School; 40 Avon St.,
Keene, NH 03431-3516; (603) 357-3122

Wilderness Society
900 17th St. NW, Washington, D.C. 20006-2596;
(202) 833-2300

Youth Groups Helping the Environment and Wildlife

Earth Force, 1908 Mount Vernon Ave., 2nd Floor, Alexandria, VA 22301; (703) 299-9400

Environmental Youth Alliance, P.O. Box 34097, Station D, Vancouver, B.C. V6J 4M1, Canada; (604) 873-0617; e-mail: ddragan@istar.ca

Foundation for the Future of Youth, 11426 Rockville Pike, Suite 100, Rockville, MD 20852; (301) 468-9431; e-mail: dpines@health.org

Free the Planet! 218 D St. SE, Washington, DC 20003; (202) 547-3656; e-mail: freetheplanet@essential.org

Global Response, P.O. Box 7490, Boulder, CO 80306-7490; (303) 444-0306; e-mail: globresponse @igc.apc.org

Global Rivers Environmental Education Network, 206 S. Fifth Ave., Suite 150, Ann Arbor, MI 48104; (313) 761-8142; e-mail: green@green.org

Kids Against Pollution, P.O. Box 22, Newport, NY 13416; (315) 845-8597; e-mail: kap@borg.com

Kids for Saving Earth Worldwide, P.O. Box 421118, Plymouth, MN 55442; (612) 559-1234; e-mail: kseww@aol.com

Kids! Renew America, 1400 16th St. NW, Suite 710, Washington, DC 20036; (202) 922-RENEW; e-mail: renewamerica@igc.apc.org

National 4-H Council, 7100 Connecticut Ave., Chevy Chase, MD 20815; (301) 961-2908; e-mail: chokis@fourhcouncil.edu

The Natural Guard, 142 Howard Ave., New Haven, CT 06519; (203) 787-0229; e-mail: tng@snet.net

Student Conservation Association, P.O. Box 550, Charlestown, NH 03603; (603) 543-1700

National Office:
United States Fish and Wildlife Service
1849 C St. NW
Washington, DC 20240
(202) 208-4717

Regional Offices of the U.S. Fish and Wildlife Service

Region 1: Pacific Regional Office
(CA, HI, and Pacific Islands, ID, NV, or WA)
Eastside Federal Complex
911 NE 11th Ave.
Portland, OR 97232-4181
(503) 231-6118

Region 2: Southwest Regional Office
(AZ, MN, OK, TX)
500 Gold Avenue SW
Room 3018
Albuquerque, NM 87102
(508) 248-6282

Region 3: Great Lakes/Big Rivers Regional Office (IA, IL, IN, MI, MN, MO, OH, WI)
1 Federal Dr.
Federal Building
Fort Snelling, MN 55111
(612) 725-3563

Region 4: Southeast Regional Office
(FL, GA, KY, LA, MS, NC, PR, SC, TN, VI)
1875 Century Blvd.
Atlanta, GA 30345
(404) 679-4000

Region 5: Northeast Regional Office (CT, DC, DE, MA, MD, ME, NH, NJ, PA, RI, VA, VT, WV)
300 Westgate Center Dr.
Hadley, MA 01035
(413) 253-8200

Region 6: Mountain/Prairie Regional Office
(CO, KS, MT, ND, NE, SD, UT, WY)
134 Union Blvd.
P.O. Box 25486
Denver, CO 80225
(303) 236-7920

Region 7: Alaska Regional Office (AK)
1011 East Tudor Rd.
Anchorage, AK 99503
(907) 786-3542